6-04

DATE DUE

DEMCO 128-8155

Welcome to the Ivory Tower of Babel:

Confessions of a Conservative College Professor

WELCOME TO THE IVORY TOWER OF BABEL:

Confessions of a Conservative College Professor

By
Mike S. Adams

HARBOR
HOUSE

WELCOME TO THE IVORY TOWER OF BABEL
Confessions of a Conservative College Professor
By Mike S. Adams
A Harbor House Book/2004

For information address:
        HARBOR HOUSE
        3010 STRATFORD DRIVE
        AUGUSTA, GEORGIA 30909

Jacket Design by Jane H. Carter
Author photo by Matt McGraw

Cataloging-in-Publication Data
Adams, Mike S., 1964-
Welcome to the Ivory Tower of Babel : confessions of a conservative
college professor / by Mike S. Adams.
p. cm.
ISBN 1-891799-17-7
1. Education, Higher--Political aspects--United States.
2. College teachers--United States--Attitudes. I. Title.
LC89.A542 2004
378.73--dc22

                                                        2003027508

Printed in the United States of America
10 9 8 7 6 5 4 3 2 1

Dedicated to ...

My wife Krysten.
And, of course, to an undivided humanity.

Contents

PART TWO:
An *"Out of the Closet" Conservative Speaks Out*

PART THREE:
Intellectual Terrorism in the Wake of 9/11

EPILOGUE

Thanks to . . .

First of all, my parents: Joe Adams, who taught me that tolerance for fools is not a virtue and Marilyn Adams, who told me that I was a good writer—even after I flunked high school English for the fourth year in a row. Of course, I must also thank my brother David for reading this manuscript and making me delete the *really* irreverent parts.

Virginia Rester for all her support throughout the years. She has also done a great job of dealing with my uncles, Jimmy and Johnny Rester. (Johnny told me I had better mention his name somewhere in this book).

Dr. David L. McMillen, an honest old-school liberal, who inspired me to enter the teaching profession. David used to occasionally bash President Reagan's policies in class while allowing others to bash him for doing it. He is one of a dying breed of professors who truly understand the consequences of free speech. In other words, he claims no constitutional freedom from having his feelings hurt.

Cecil Willis for supporting my First Amendment rights every step of the way. Also, for teaching me to handle lunatics with laughter, not lawsuits.

Thor Halvorrsen, Alan Kors, Greg Lukianoff, and Harvey Silverglate at the Foundation for Individual Rights in Education (FIRE) for supporting me in the court of public opinion in the wake of September 11th. Jon Sanders with the John Locke Foundation, Jody Brown with Agape Press, and Gina Delfonzo with Breakpoint Online for publishing several of my early editorials. Jon Garthwaite and Jennifer Biddison at the Heritage Foundation for giving me a wider audience for my essays on life in the academy.

Charlton Allen for telling me which portions of this manuscript would get me into trouble and then making sure I included them anyway. Randall Floyd for having confidence in me and for giving me this incredible opportunity.

Finally, to all my Leftist colleagues who have given (and continue to give) me plenty of material to laugh and write about. This manuscript is a test of their commitment to academic freedom.

Introduction

August 28, 2003:

Welcome to my book about the "Ivory Tower of Babel." Before we get started, let me warn you that this will probably be the shortest book introduction you ever read. I don't have much time to write because, as we speak, a feminist professor is combing the halls removing "offensive" flyers from all of the bulletin boards in the Social Science building here at UNC-Wilmington. I just saw her remove a couple of "Hooters" flyers along with several ads for upcoming fraternity parties. She thinks it's her job to remove all speech from the building that is potentially offensive or degrading to women. She has tenure so she has plenty of time to donate to the campus "thought" police. I'm going to go see if she removes that "Queers for Christ" flyer as soon as I'm finished writing this introduction. It's a pretty safe bet that she won't touch it.

Political correctness has been a problem ever since I started teaching here ten years ago. It became an even bigger problem when the administration started calling it the "diversity movement" a few years later. Shortly after they gave the movement a name and official status, a flurry of programs, offices, and initiatives began to emerge--all in the name of campus diversity. Throughout this book, I will argue that this movement has actually reduced the amount of diversity on campus. I will also talk about some grave threats the movement now poses to the First Amendment. But before I begin to talk about how the university has changed, I have to say something about how I have changed over the last ten years. Indeed, it is the combination of the fact that the university has moved solidly in one direction, and I in another, that is responsible for this book.

When I arrived at UNC-Wilmington in 1993, I was a Democrat and an atheist. I had voted for Michael Dukakis in 1988 and Bill Clinton in 1992. I had also fully renounced religion in April of 1992 after several years as an agnostic. Fortunately, in March of 1996, a trip to a prison in Quito, Ecuador caused me to renounce both atheism and agnosticism. That decision followed a conversation with a Catholic prisoner who had been awaiting his trial for two years. He told me that if he ever got a trial and was convicted, his sentence would be about two months. That prisoner taught me something about thankfulness. He also taught me that sometimes there's a reason people find themselves in places they don't want to be. I would have thanked that prisoner in my acknowledgments, but I don't even know his name.

Later, in December of 1999, I visited a mentally retarded inmate on Texas' death row. He had raped two women and murdered one. He also quoted John 3:16 to me during our visit. For some reason, the visit inspired me to buy a copy of the King James Bible with the intention of reading it from cover to cover. By the time I finished, I had joined a church and switched to the Republican Party. I should also mention that, by this time, I had tenure. All of these things help to explain why I am such an outspoken critic of the campus political and moral climate.

In the fall of 2001, my outspoken conservatism finally got me into a bit of trouble at UNCW. After a student blamed the terror attacks of 911 on the United States, I had the audacity to label her speech as "bigoted," "unintelligent," and "immature." As a result, she accused me of "libel." When the university read some of my personal e-mails at her request (searching for evidence of "libel"), a First Amendment and e-mail privacy controversy erupted. In an effort to control a public relations disaster, the university lied to a national reporter when he asked whether they had read any of my e-mails. Later, they also lied about the fact that they had turned over records of my e-mail correspondence to my socialist accuser. Around that time, I decided to write this book.

The theme of the book is pretty straightforward. It is simply a look at life at the modern (or should I say, postmodern) university through the eyes of a conservative professor. That alone makes the book unique as there are few "out of the closet" conservatives on our nation's campuses. The title's reference to the Tower of Babel story from the Book of Genesis is also a reference to the Utopian mind-set that dominates most universities today. It is also a nice way of saying that most of my colleagues are socialists.

I also believe that most campuses are in a state of turmoil not unlike the conclusion of that famous story in Genesis. In other words, I think that socialism has failed and that its proponents are in a bit of a frenzy as a consequence. Some call this the multi-cultural era on our nation's campuses. Others call it the postmodern era. I call it chaos, because everyone seems to be speaking a different language. And, sadly, there is little interest in universal truths or principles in academia today.

There isn't much need for further elaboration on the theme of this book. The average reader will quickly ascertain it. While it is a serious book in many ways, you will undoubtedly find yourself laughing in most parts. Indeed, most of these stories will seem too strange to be true, especially for those who have never worked in academia.

In the first part of the book, you will read a number of letters I wrote, mostly to members of the university community. While most of these letters were never sent, they were written principally to help me preserve a record of my life in academia as I became disillusioned with the university climate. I did not have tenure when I wrote most of these letters. That explains why few were actually sent.

The second part of the book is a collection of editorials I have published, mostly on various Internet Web magazines. The courage to write these opinions can be explained by two factors. First, I had tenure by the time they were written. Second, I had been given a green light from the university to speak out on "any issue whatsoever" after the aforementioned e-mail scandal. That green light was issued after the university was accused of censoring me for my political beliefs. My chronicles of that scandal comprise part three of the manuscript. It is a shocking testament to the status of civil liberties and free speech at the modern university. When you read it, I suspect that you will agree with my assertion that political correctness is simply out of control in academia.

Without any further delay, I would like to get started. I hope you enjoy reading this as much as I enjoyed writing it. And, most of all, I hope that, after another ten years of teaching, there is not enough material for a sequel. If there is, everyone is in deep trouble. Well, not everyone. The feminists and the "Queers for Christ" will be just fine, I'm sure.

PART ONE

Letters From A
Disillusioned Professor

A Left Wing "Debate" On Affirmative Action

Dear Director of Diversity:

I was absolutely thrilled when I recently saw flyers on campus suggesting that the university was sponsoring a debate on the issue of affirmative action. This has been an issue of great concern to me ever since I first sat in on a university search committee meeting during my first semester as a professor.

That meeting took place in the faculty lunchroom with members of a committee who were assembled to select a new social work professor. About ten minutes into the meeting, I was shocked to hear a committee member object to a candidate she had previously met at a conference by saying that he was "a little too white male" for the position. She also stated that another candidate was probably "too religious" to be a professor, noting that the candidate had previously attended several "overtly religious" schools.

I have also been perplexed by some of the visits our department has received from the director of Human Resources. I know that one time he came to the department to give us helpful hints on how to identify blacks and other minority candidates in our pool. I guess that was supposed to help us eliminate discrimination from the hiring process. Of course, we don't always need any help identifying minority applicants. For example, one minority candidate recently sent a picture of herself lecturing at the podium along with her application. Perhaps she did this to let us see what she looked like in action, rather than to call attention to her status as a black female.

I also wondered at first why the Human Resources director contacted us during one of our searches to say that one of our alternates was a black female. I understood things better when we were politely asked to bump her up on the list in order to have a more "diverse" interview pool. I must admit that I laughed hysterically when I went to pick the woman up at the airport and saw that she was a white female in her late fifties. She would explain to me in the interview that she was "part African-American, 20 percent approximately," and that she grew up in a black neighborhood. I didn't know whether to accuse her of lying or thank her for shedding light on the absurdity of our affirmative action policies. While the other faculty members were mad, I thought the university got what it deserved. After all, we can't accuse her of lying on her application if we also lied on the application by saying "UNCW does not discriminate on the basis of race."

I think that the kinds of things I have described above would have been great to bring up in the affirmative action "debate" that the university recently hosted. However, when I attended the debate, I noticed that law professor, Adrian Wing, a black female who supported affirmative action, was the only one speaking at the "debate." Her speech began with an argument that defenders of affirmative action usually fall back on as a last resort; namely, that affirmative action is something that whites owe to minorities.

Professor Wing first asked the audience how many considered themselves to be members of the upper class. She then asked how many owned property. Her point was that the Framers of the Constitution were upper class white males who owned property and were different from the average person in the audience. Next, she boldly stated that since "they" had made "their" own laws for "their" own benefit, it was time for "us" to have some of "our" own laws to help destroy the persistent inequality that has been present throughout American history.

Of course, if it really was the case that the Constitution was written by rich white males for their own personal benefit, that wouldn't necessarily lead to the conclusion that other groups have the right to establish their own self-serving laws in an effort to restore equity. As a professor who teaches criminal procedure, and who has authored a book on the subject, I cover United States Supreme Court decisions on a daily basis. Rarely, does one hear of a case in which a wealthy white male successfully relies upon our constitution to attain justice. The overwhelming majority of those who rely on our constitution are poor and non-white.

Later in the "debate," Professor Wing simply stood at the podium and read a long list of objections to affirmative action and dismissed them all as "myths." She then concluded that there were no legitimate reasons to object to affirmative action. Next, she tried to provide reasons *for* affirmative action. Towards that end, she first quoted statistics on the percentage of minority families headed by single mothers. Then, she talked about the problem of violent crime victimization among minorities. Together, these two issues formed the heart of her argument.

I agreed with Wing's specific assertion that too many black females are raising children on their own. I was already aware of (and concerned about) the 70 percent illegitimacy rate in the black community. But it seemed to me that the massive increase in illegitimacy rates following the Great Society's "war on poverty" might lead some reasonable people to conclude that social programs were a part of the problem rather than part of the solution. Perhaps this would have come up in a real debate.

When Wing shifted to the topic of crime, she cited two specific examples of minority victimization, which, for her, accentuated the need for affirmative action. Whites against minorities perpetrated both. The first was the Rodney King beating in Los Angeles. The second was the James Byrd murder in Jasper, Texas in 1998. Wing made no mention of the fact that other minorities commit 80 percent of all crimes committed against minorities. Nor did she mention that there are over eight violent crimes committed by minorities against whites for every one committed by whites against minorities. Perhaps these statistics would have come out in an actual debate on the issue.

I know this letter is getting long and that you have better things to do than to listen to my objections to affirmative action, so I will conclude with a simple request. Could you bring Professor Wing back to campus and allow me to have a real debate with her on affirmative action? I know she charges a hefty fee to "debate" on affirmative action. But the good news is that I won't charge a dime. I guess that would be another example of affirmative action. And wouldn't it also be a real example of a debate? Please let me know if you are interested. And thanks for listening.

Answering A False Accusation of Racism

====================

Dear Falsely Accused Racist:

I would like to start off by expressing my deepest sympathies concerning the recent false accusation of racism, which has been levied against you publicly by another professor at our university. I know that this is especially difficult to deal with as a first year professor without tenure. I am also glad that you have written me requesting advice on this matter. I hope that you will forgive my lengthy response to your request as I have much to say on this subject.

For a number of years, I have been perplexed by the difficulty that many academics have with the proper use of such simple terms as racism, prejudice, discrimination, and stereotyping. They are always getting them confused, while the terms are really quite simple. Racism is just the belief that some races are naturally, or innately, superior (or inferior) to others. Once one understands that concept, differentiating between the other three terms is as easy as learning your ABCs. I mean that literally because, "A" stands for attitude, "B" stands for behavior, and "C" stands for cognition. Prejudice deals with negative attitudes (e.g., "I don't like whites."). Discrimination deals with negative behavior (e.g., "I won't hire blacks."). Stereotyping deals with negative cognitive beliefs (e.g., "I think Southerners are lazy."). Since these terms are so simple, I have come to conclude that most of the "confusion" about their meaning is intentional.

One of the best books I have ever read dealing with the topic of racism is William Wilbanks' *Myth of a Racist Criminal Justice System*, published in 1987. The part of the book that is relevant to our discussion is found in chapter two. In just one simple paragraph, Wilbanks shows how one can expose someone who is making a false accusation of racism. During my second year at UNCW, Wilbanks' advice came in very handy. I'll try to make it brief.

On a Wednesday afternoon in November of 1994, I was having lunch with five of my UNCW colleagues. There were about 25 people total in the faculty lunchroom that day. All of them were Democrats. This was the day after the Democratic Party had lost control of the House of Representatives for the first time in decades. A social work professor was seated across from me. It was his first year at the university and only my second. He was in his early fifties, had served in Vietnam, and was usually trying to convince his colleagues that he was more liberal than they were on any number of social issues. By now, I'm sure you know whom I'm talking about.

Though normally a very compassionate and caring man, he tends to take offense at strange things. He also likes to tell whites what black people think about a variety of social issues. I have always thought it was a little racist for white men to defend minorities and make their arguments for them, but I never said anything to him about it. I don't like to call people racists.

In the midst of our discussion about the previous day's elections, he paused from his lengthy diatribe against new House Speaker Newt Gingrich to lament the fact that California voters had voted to pass Proposition 187. In case you don't recall, this was a measure that denied welfare benefits and other forms of government assistance to the families of illegal immigrants. Another faculty member joined in to express her amazement at the wide margin by which it passed.

Suddenly, I looked up and said, "If I were a Californian, I would have voted for it, too." One of the professors seated at the table happened to be from Argentina. She asked me why I would support such a measure. I said, "Well, I'm from Texas and ..." Before I could finish my sentence, she asked, "Well, what does that mean?" Then, my friend in Social Work shouted out (in the midst of all of my colleagues) "It means he's a racist! That's what it means!"

After his outburst, I just sat back and waited for the anger to pass, thinking that one of my colleagues would rush to my defense. No such thing happened. We all just sat there in silence. Later, a colleague would say to me privately that my accuser was out of line. Of course, I wasn't going to let him have the last word.

I looked for an opportunity to talk to him about the incident over the next several days when I went to the faculty lunchroom. When I did not get a chance to speak to him alone, I decided to e-mail two simple questions that William Wilbanks recommends as a means of exposing someone who is making a false accusation of racism. First, I asked, "What is your definition of racism?" Second, I asked, "How exactly did it apply to the issue we were discussing?" I also added that I was disappointed in his negative characterization of me in front of my colleagues. He responded by saying that he would be glad to have lunch with me sometime to explain what racism meant to him. In other words, he didn't really know offhand. In fact, he never gave me a definition. But he did apologize. And he hasn't called me a racist since then.

Now, let's move on to your dilemma. Unless I am mistaken, the facts of your situation can be roughly summarized as follows: The other day at lunch, you went to put your lunch tray down on a table that a minority staff member had just left. When you saw him approach the table again with his dessert you realized that you had taken his seat. You immediately apologized and offered to move. He told you to sit back down and quietly moved to another table. You ate the rest of your meal and then proceeded to go back to your office.

Later that afternoon, I understand that you got an e-mail message from a black female professor, coincidentally a social work professor. It seems that she had seen the entire "incident" with the staff member and wrote to express her distaste at your racist "takeover" of the man's seat. I understand that she then stated that she had always heard that UNCW was a "racist institution" and that now she knew why.

I can certainly understand why you called the staff member to apologize. That was smart, and I am glad that he assured you that he knew it was an accident and said that he wasn't angry. But now that you have tried to relay this information to the social work professor, and she has refused to listen and stated that she didn't care if he was offended or not, you need to take the offensive. I don't want to upset you, but I just found out that she is discussing the incident in her social work classes as an example of racism.

I would strongly urge you to write your accuser immediately and ask her those same two questions I asked the person who falsely accused me of racism. Since you are a known supporter of the campus diversity movement and a gay activist, you shouldn't have trouble beating this accusation.

If, by any chance, she tries to turn the question around and ask for your definition of racism, here is my advice. Remember that both of you were hired by UNCW on exactly the same day. Tell her that as a white female in Sociology, you received your doctoral degree several years *before* accepting your position and had already been teaching at the college level for ten years. Then remind her that she, as a black female in Social Work, had been teaching for five years when she was hired and that she had not formally received her doctorate. Then inform her that she received a starting salary $8,000 higher than you. You may also want to throw in the fact that she was given a salary higher than two tenured white male professors in her department.

Certainly, she will be able to see that you are the true victim of racial discrimination at UNCW. That should be enough to get her off your back. If not, please don't hesitate to call or write to me again. Although we have very different political views, I will be glad to help defend you against this baseless accusation.

A Tale of Two Feminists

Dear Director of Human Resources:

I am writing confidentially to solicit your advice on a personnel issue of grave concern both to me and to some of my colleagues. Recently, an untenured faculty member came into my office in a rare state of excitement. Because he rarely shows his emotions, I had a feeling that something was really wrong.

After shutting the door to my office, I was very surprised when he proceeded to tell me that an untenured female professor had just complained to him that the only other untenured female professor in our department had just "stolen her boyfriend." At first glance, this doesn't seem like an important matter requiring a trip to my office (or a letter to you, for that matter). However, the person that the two women were apparently fighting over was, at the time, a candidate for a job in our department. Naturally, my colleague was shocked. If the accusation was true, both professors were exercising horrendous professional judgment.

Although I had hoped that the story was false, it appears that it is not, because I have now heard a consistent story from one of our undergraduate students. Apparently, one of the two quarreling women (his advisor) told him they had a confrontation at the hotel where the candidate was staying on his recent job interview. It seems that both of them had decided to pay him a little visit at exactly the same time. I know that we go to great lengths to make our candidates comfortable, but this is probably going too far. What do you think?

I am troubled by more than just the question of whether this inappropriate behavior has taken place. I am also troubled that one of the professors involved is so willing to discuss it publicly. It seems that she is making no effort to conceal what has transpired. Do they think that the rules prohibiting "amorous" relationships (where there is an obvious conflict of interest) simply do not apply to them? In not, why? Do they only apply to men? It is all the more remarkable given that neither of them have tenure.

I deeply regret not writing you sooner. The events I have described happened in April. Now, as we near the end of December, the conflict between the two feminists seems to have escalated At the recent faculty Christmas party hosted by Chancellor Leutze, one of the women publicly accused the other of being addicted to cocaine. I am certain that the charges are a baseless attempt to retaliate for what the accuser saw as an attempt to "steal her boyfriend." Fortunately, another professor relayed the story to the accused party who, quite justifiably, reported it to the department chair. However, there has been no formal disciplinary action taken in conjunction with any of these events.

I know this is a lot to put on you at once. Please contact me if you need more information. While I am not sure of the appropriate course of action, I am sure that we agree on one thing. The matter simply cannot be ignored.

Rotten Meat and Ethnocentrism

Dear Mr. Colson:

I recently read an account of one of your visits to a men's prison in Quito, Ecuador. I was pleased to read of your account because I have had the opportunity to visit a different men's prison in Quito. I wanted to first share my prison experience with you and then tell you about the difficulties I had trying to publicize the human rights abuses that I witnessed there. It may shock you to hear that most of my problems getting the word out came at the hands of self-described liberals.

In 1996, I participated in a teaching exchange program that my university had arranged with San Francisco University just outside of Quito. While I was on that exchange, a chance meeting with a law student in Quito resulted in an invitation to visit a men's prison, where I would learn firsthand about human rights abuses in Ecuador's system of justice. The student, who was doing some human rights work in the prison, happened to be friends with the family with whom I was staying. When she offered to take me to the prison, I was naturally elated.

Of course, I was a little less elated after being robbed on the bus on the way to the prison. Nonetheless, we got out in one of the worst parts of town, just beneath a statue of the Virgin Mary poised on a hill across from the prison. We then crossed the street to the gates of the prison where several guards were armed with machine guns. When they let us in the prison, I made sure that they stamped "visitas" on my hand twice just for safe measure.

A young prisoner by the name of Pedro Castello met us at the gate and took us back to the warden's chambers. Pedro was 21 when he was arrested for allegedly forging his passport. He had just been acquitted after a yearlong trial that started three years after he was arrested. He was waiting for his family to raise money to pay his court fees before the prison would release him. He was then 25 years old.

The warden, who was surprisingly friendly, expressed no objection to allowing me to tour the prison. He was even willing to send two of his prison guards with me. This was no small gesture as there were only ten of them assigned to watch over a prison population of one thousand. Our tour began on the outer perimeter of the prison with visits to the library, the barbershop, and a woodwork shop. Things got more interesting when we went through another set of gates into the heart of the prison where most of the inmates were housed. When they opened the gates, the smell of body odor, human waste, and rotting food was almost unbearable.

It was almost as difficult to adjust to the sights as to the smells of the prison. Puddles of urine and fecal matter were visible as were prisoners with open scars, some from fights, and others from suicide attempts. When the guards took me inside one of the cells, I better understood the origins of these visible wounds.

Most of the cells were open so that prisoners could roam freely about the prison. However, one cell containing almost fifty inmates was closed and locked. Its inhabitants were classified as among the prison's most dangerous offenders. My request to enter the cell and speak to those inmates was granted. They seemed glad to see someone from the outside. Although packed into only about thirty-six square meters, they quickly woke a prisoner to make room for me to sit on one of the bunks. They were cordial enough to make me feel at ease, despite the fact that a large butcher knife was sitting right in front of me on the top of a broken thirteen-inch television set. After a few minutes of questioning, we toured the rest of the bottom floor where the poorest prisoners stayed. Rent was less than a dollar a week downstairs. The prisoners' relatives begged outside the prison gates for the money.

Within minutes, I got an idea of what happened to those who did not pay their rent. On the way to the kitchen, we passed through a small room that appeared to be used to wash food before bringing it into the kitchen area for preparation. In the corner of the room, a guard was beating a prisoner mercilessly with a large club until one of our escorting guards shouted "tenemos visitas, pare" which, by the way, does not translate into "stop, you're violating that man's constitutional rights." He did stop the beating before dragging the trembling man from the room. As he passed, he looked at me as if to say "good timing." He didn't look a day over eighteen.

We hurriedly passed through the kitchen due to the excessive heat, as well as the unpleasant odor of the food. Anyone who has been to South America has seen the little shacks on the side of the road with pigs hanging from the front porches from which the owner cuts and cooks meat on the spot for customers. Sometimes, early in the morning you can drive by one of these places and see a pig that has been hanging there overnight as it is about to be used again for the second straight day. I was told that eventually these leftovers made it to the prisoners. This explains both the odor and the practice of boiling the meat before giving it to the prisoners.

I was pleased to make it upstairs to the "nicer" part of the prison where the higher rent, still less than two dollars a week, bought prisoners the right to keep personal items in their cells and to have relatives bring in clean clothes from time to time. The clothes of some prisoners housed downstairs were rotting off of their bodies. Also, upstairs inmates only had to share a room with about twenty other prisoners. After a brief tour, I had a chance to talk to four prisoners who were working together with the law students at the Catholic University towards the improvement of prison conditions.

Despite the fact that the guards were present with us, the discussion was frank and open. I learned a few interesting things about the system, including the fact that murder carried a maximum sentence of only sixteen years while drug possession carried a minimum of 25 years. The guards estimated that 80 percent of the prisoners there had not been tried and would wait an average of three years for their trial to begin. Some of those trials would take five years to complete in a system where there were no juries and almost no defense attorneys. Furthermore, all legal motions were written. The guards would also admit that prisoners were occasionally shot in the back after being told they were free to go. Such incidents would be reported as thwarted escape attempts. Thus, there was really no need to formally bring back the death penalty.

Before I walked out of that prison, a man who had been awaiting trial for larceny for two years thanked me for visiting and showing concern for the prisoners. I was surprised by his display of religious faith since he had already been in prison awaiting trial for longer than his sentence would have been had he been convicted. He also had two small children.

When I stepped out into the streets of Quito, I looked up at the statue of the Virgin Mary and thought about how people in my own country have so much to be thankful for and yet try so hard to find ways to be unhappy, to be offended, and to be seen as victims. So many true victims in that prison found ways to be thankful and to have faith in the face of hopelessness.

I went back to my friend's apartment and immediately began to write about everything I had seen, hoping to publish an account of my visit which might somehow be used to improve the plight of those inside the gates of the Ecuadorian prisons. After returning to the United States, I finished the article and submitted it to a journal called "Humanity and Society." The reviewers recommended its publication, and the editor informed me that the article would be published in the next issue. I was excited, as it seemed that the piece was being rushed to the presses.

When the article did not come out in the issue in which it was supposed to appear, I contacted the journal's editor, Michelle Stone, a sociologist from Youngstown State University. She informed me that she had reversed her decision to publish the manuscript after giving it a careful reading. Her reasons were twofold. First, she said it "wasn't nice to criticize the foods of cultures other than our own." Second, she said that she didn't like a reference I had made in the paper concerning "Charles Colson's religious program."

I tried to explain to her that the comment I made in the article about the food smelling bad was made *after* I explained that the meat being served to the prisoners was, in fact, rotten. I insisted that rotten meat was considered to be bad universally. It really wasn't a case of imposing my Western values on another culture. Nonetheless, she insisted that I was being ethnocentric.

With regard to the remark about your fellowship program, I must admit that I didn't even try to change her mind. I don't know whether it was your previous association with the Nixon White House, or just the fact that you are a Baptist advocating prison reforms based on Biblical principles (rather than Marxist principles), that makes her so angry. God is clearly more forgiving than liberal professors. I suppose that's all that counts.

Fortunately, several months later "Humanity and Society" got a new editor. When I called him and explained the situation, he agreed to publish the article upon written proof of its prior acceptance. The article was published nine months later than originally planned. Eventually, a congresswoman from Florida read a copy of my article and spoke with representatives of Amnesty International. She then boarded a plane to Ecuador to free an American woman wrongfully held in a prison in the very city I had written about. She recognized the urgency of the plight of those prisoners. That sense of urgency was lost on Professor Stone. She was too busy being sensitive to the cooks.

An Illegitimate Attack

Dear Chris:

I wanted to thank you for coming by the office today to share your concerns about what happened earlier this week in your social work class. I also wanted to apologize for what you experienced at the hands of your follow classmates. And I certainly would like to talk more about how your professor handled the situation you described to me. In my opinion, no student should ever be subjected to the kind of personal attack you described simply for expressing his constitutionally protected opinion. Moreover, I think your opinion has a sound basis in fact.

Let me state first of all that the issue you were discussing—the pros and cons of interracial adoption—is an important social issue which is routinely discussed in sociology and social work classes around the country. However, that does not mean the topic is given fair treatment in most of these classes.

Indeed, the fact that sociology and social work professors are
so overwhelmingly liberal tends to affect the balance of these
kinds of discussions. Therefore, I wasn't surprised that your
professor expressed such a strong opposition to interracial
adoption on the grounds that black children needed to be
raised by those "capable" of teaching them about the "legacy
of individual and institutional racism" in America. Nor am I
surprised that most of the students in your class merely par-
roted the opinions of the professor.

I *am* surprised (pleasantly) that you had the courage to say
that you believed that interracial adoptions were necessary on
the basis of the discrepancy between black and white illegitimacy rates. I believe you said that the fact that "most black
children are illegitimate" must be taken into consideration in
resolving this complex issue. Of course, that was around the
time your classmates attacked you with accusations of
"racism" and "insensitivity."

First of all, Chris, just ignore the remarks about insensitivity.
You need to focus on the accusations of racism. Those accusations will not be hard to rebut. If you simply ask those classmates
to define racism—which is, of course, "a belief that some races
are by nature superior to others"—they will probably fall silent.
If they do define the term correctly, all you have to do is ask them
how it applies to the remarks you made in class. There is no way
that they will be able to prevail if you take this rational approach.

The real issue, of course, is how you deal with your professor. If I understood you correctly, you said that she simply sat
back and laughed while the other students hurled these baseless accusations. Here's how I want you to deal with her:

When you return to class next week, raise your hand and ask
the professor to quote the exact rate of black illegitimacy in
America. That figure is 70 percent, by the way. If she says she
doesn't know, ask her how a PhD in Social Work could "not

know" such a basic statistic. If she says she does know, then you have her nailed. That means that she *was aware* that most black children are illegitimate, but chose to pretend that she wasn't while you were being attacked personally. In other words, she allowed you to be accused of racism rather than take a risk that she would be accused of racism for standing up for you.

Simply put, your professor is either a) ignorant or, b) cowardly. You need to call her on it. And don't worry about retaliation, Chris. I've done my homework and I know that your professor doesn't have tenure. I promise that I will provide you with a free lawyer if she retaliates with her grade book. But she won't do that if she hears the word "lawsuit." Right now, she's betting that she can intimidate you, because students rarely stand up to this kind of intellectual terrorism. But when students do stand up for themselves, they learn that all terrorists (intellectual or otherwise) are cowards.

I know that the prospect of playing hardball with one of your professors is a little unsettling. Nonetheless, I would encourage you to think about the consequences of remaining silent when speaking up is the right thing to do. After all, that's the reason you lost respect for your professor. Don't make the same mistake, Chris. Your parents aren't spending tens of thousands of dollars on your education for you to be branded as a racist for telling the truth. Nor is your professor being paid to suppress the truth in order to enhance the self-esteem of minorities and advance her political agenda.

Think about what I've said and make sure you do the right thing.

Cornel West and Friends

Dear Professor West:

I have been trying to get in touch with you for several days, but haven't had much luck. First, an e-mail I sent you bounced back with an automated response indicating that you do not read, write, or answer e-mail. I also called your secretary who informed me that you have been out of your office lately. Therefore, I thought I would write with a few quick questions inspired by a conversation I recently had with an untenured colleague. He takes offense that our university has invited you to speak on our campus because he thinks that you are an anti-Semite. I just want to get some information from you before I decide whether I agree.

The first time I heard you speak, you were sitting on a panel on a cable television broadcast. Although it was many years ago, I believe you were discussing various racial issues, such as affirmative action. I also remember that you were seated next to Khalid Abdul Muhammad of the Nation of Islam. On the phone, your secretary confirmed that you and Khalid were friends and that you had made various public appearances together.

When I saw you on television with Muhammad, I immediately remembered a speech he had delivered in 1993 at Keane College, during which he said the following:

> *If the white man don't get out of town by sundown, we kill everything white in South Africa. We kill the women; we kill the children; we kill the babies. We kill the faggot; we kill the lesbian; we kill them all.*

Muhammad also said the following about Jews:

> *The so-called Jew is a European strain of people who crawled around on all fours in the caves and hills of Europe, eating juniper roots and eating each other. You (Jews) slept with your dead for 2000 years, smelling the stench coming up from the decomposing body. You slept in your urination and your defecation . . . The so-called Jews are bloodsuckers of the black nation . . . That's why you call yourself Rubenstein, Goldstein and Silverstein, because you've been stealing rubies and gold and silver all over the earth ... Everybody talks about Hitler exterminating six million Jews. That's right. But don't nobody talk about what they do to Hitler.*

It struck me as odd that you would appear on national television seated next to such a virulent racist. At the time, you were a Harvard professor, a widely read author, and had spoken more than once at my university. Even back then, I wondered why we would pay for a speaker who made public appearances with genocidal racists like Muhammad. Not long after that, I decided to go to the library to search for some of your publications.

When I got to the library I noticed that you had collaborated on a publication with a noted feminist professor named Bell Hooks. I immediately remembered reading an essay by Hooks in which she described an unfortunate incident on an airplane. She was sitting in first-class with a friend (whom she referred to only as "K") when a white man approached with a boarding pass assigned to the seat in which "K" was sitting. An attendant informed "K" that her upgrade to first-class had not been completed and that it was too late to fix it. "K" then moved to coach. The white man sat down in the seat actually assigned to him and apologized to Hooks, who rejected his apology and accused him of both racism and sexism. She then proceeded to pen the following: "I am writing this essay sitting beside an anonymous white male that I long to murder." It seems like a lot of your friends want to kill people because of the color of their skin. Doesn't that bother you?

Later, I came across a library entry for a book you had written, called *Race Matters*. I checked out the book and started reading the following sentence that appears on page three: "What happened in Los Angeles in April of 1992 was neither a race riot nor a class rebellion." I immediately began to think about all of the whites that were dragged out of their cars and beaten solely on the basis of their race. Reginald Denny, the truck driver who was kicked, beaten, and nearly killed by a cinder block that was repeatedly dropped on his head, was the first to come to mind.

I then read the next sentence that said, "Rather, this monumental upheaval was a multi-racial, trans-class, and largely male display of justified social rage." That was all I needed to hear. In my opinion, no one who refers to racially motivated violence as "justified" is worth reading. I would greatly appreciate if you would write back to tell me where I am wrong.

A few years later, I caught an interview you did on the *O'Reilly Factor* shortly after the controversial 2000 Presidential election. The show's host, Bill O'Reilly, responded to a comment you made about black voter disenfranchisement by asking you whether voting machines in Florida could tell the difference between white and non-white voters. In other words, were the machines capable of somehow spotting black voters and then rejecting only their votes. I noticed that you never answered the question. You just urged viewers to consider the "fact" that those machines were built and put in place in a state with a long history of white supremacy and lynching.

Later, O'Reilly asked you about your alliance with Reverend Al Sharpton, who is perhaps best known for his support of Tawana Brawley. As you already know, Brawley made national headlines when she claimed that she had been raped by three white men, who then smeared her with excrement and wrote "KKK" and "n**ger" all over her body. After a New York grand jury concluded that she fabricated the story, Sharpton continued to echo her discredited claims. Although Sharpton himself was later sued for his comments and continues to pay damages, I noticed that you continue to be one of the biggest supporters of his bid for the Presidency. In the interview, you also refused to admit that Brawley was lying. I believe you said that the grand jury's decision was one view of what happened, but not the only view.

After seeing your interview on the *Factor*, I decided to pick up another of your books in order to better understand your perspective on racial matters. As I sat in my office reading your book, entitled *Keeping Faith*, I had a hard time understanding what you were saying. For example, I found the following passage hard to comprehend:

Following the model of the black diaspora traditions of music, athletics, and rhetoric, black cultural workers must constitute and sustain discursive and institutional networks that deconstruct earlier modern black strategies for identity-formation, demystify power relations that incorporate class, patriarchal, and homophobic biases, and construct more multivalent and multidimensional responses that articulate the complexity and diversity of black practices in the modern and postmodern world.

Reacquainting myself with your writings raised some of my old questions about you. For example, why do you make public appearances and co-author articles with racists and anti-Semites? Why can't you just say that a voting machine can't think, let alone conspire against minorities? And why can't you just admit that Tawana Brawley was lying?

After returning *Keeping Faith* to the library, I thought of some new questions. Perhaps most importantly, I wondered why (in the midst of a state budget crisis and tuition hikes) UNCW paid you $12,000 to speak recently? I have many other questions but I know you are busy. Perhaps you can write when you get back to the office. I would love to hear your "deconstruction" of my narrative. I look forward to hearing from you.

One Flew Over the Cuckoo's Desk

Dear Director of Human Resources:

I hope you have a few spare minutes because you are not going to believe this one. I know that you're busy but it would be wrong to keep this information from you. I think you may also be legally obligated to conduct some sort of investigation into the allegations I am about to share with you.

The first week of December I went to my mailbox and found the following memo:

> *December 2, 1999*
>
> *To My Colleagues in the Department of Sociology, Anthropology, & Criminal Justice:*
>
> *You have been asked to debate the possibility of giving Dr. Cecil Willis another four-year term as Chair of our department. Unfortunately, I will be able to attend today's meet-*

ing because of my Faculty Senate duties. However, I have important information concerning Cecil's qualifications and some questions about his prior actions that should be answered in open forum before you make this decision. I would therefore like to request that you either postpone today's discussion or schedule a second meeting where his candidacy would be the sole topic of discussion.

Thank you very much for your help and attention to this matter.

Sincerely,
Lynne L. Snowden

As you can imagine, this memo was the talk of the department for the rest of the day. When the department met that afternoon, we debated whether one faculty member could postpone such an important meeting on such short notice. But Cecil graciously agreed to have that second meeting, where his candidacy would be the "sole focus" of discussion.

When we reconvened on December 16, about two dozen sociologists, anthropologists, and criminologists sat awaiting the entry of Dr. Snowden, our faculty senate president. When she made her entrance, she had copies of a series of accusations printed out for everyone present. The materials she distributed are reproduced below in their entirety:

To my colleagues in the Department of Sociology, Anthropology, & Criminal Justice:

Today I wish to bring information concerning our Chair, Cecil Willis, to you. In part, I do this because I have studied hate crime and discrimination for more than 15 years, and I know the only way to stop such behavior is to confront it and bring it out in the open. Another reason is the ever changing legal structure which surrounds harassment, and finally Cecil's behavior toward me seems to be growing worse and has become a personal burden which I can no longer bear alone.

Please understand that I only wish to bring this matter to your attention. It is very difficult for me to recommend a course of action because, if Cecil is not re-elected as Chair, it is more probable that he will retaliate against me than if he is. There are three matters that should be discussed:

1. Two women, who are no longer with the department, reported to me that (sic) experienced harassment from Cecil. While I do not wish to speak for them, it is necessary that you understand I am the third such case in as many years.

2. Recently, I and a colleague wrote a paper on sexual harassment that will be published next year in the Police Chief. In going through the literature, I found that all of us could be held vicariously liable iif (sic) an employee is the "target of crude and offensive sexually harassing behaivor (sic) and has a policy of prohibiting such conduct" (Gunta & Peters, 1998). As Faculty Senate President, I could certainly be held liable if I hid such information from you when a meeting had been scheduled expressly for the purpose of discussing Cecil's fitness to remain in office.

3. Following my statement, I have listed examples of the things that have occurred in the workplace since I went up for tenure two years ago. Some of them by Cecil, some at the hands of person's (sic) yet unknown, although the police are still investigating the matter. Please realize that I believe, as a criminal justice professional, that it is always better to help people control themselves rather than to impose force from the outside. This situation is a problem that we should solve ourselves. For your information I have also attached the first 2 pages of an article which defines various protected classes and contains the reasons why I feel my experiences are harassment.

We all sat in stunned silence after hearing Snowden read her memo openly accusing Cecil of sexual harassment. In addition to foregoing the normal procedures, she had just informed us that she had been to the police under the theory that his behavior was also criminal. The evidence she claimed to have, suggesting that Willis was both a "chronic sexual harasser" and a "hate criminal," was on the last page of her handout, which she went over point by point in front of everyone. I have reproduced it below:

<u>Cecil</u>

1. Use of crude hand gestures with a sexual nature
2. Threatening lack of promotion
3. Making false statements regarding promotion
4. Developing policies which only applied to me, such as only 2 DIS (Directed Individual Study projects) per semester
5. Lack of support for publication efforts
6. Using false information in my annual evaluation
7. Trying to humiliate me in front of my colleagues

<u>Persons Unknown</u>

1. Mutilation of Watchband in my office
2. Destruction of tenure documents
3. Tampering with computer, including:
    - erasing bookmarks
    - insertion of derogatory files
    - manipulation of margins
    - attempted crashes of computer
    - etc., etc.
4. Tampering with printer
5. Note found in car

As you can imagine, the atmosphere in that room was surreal when Snowden began explaining all of the accusations on that final page. I stopped her after the first point to ask for an example of a crude hand gesture. She politely asked me to save my questions until the end. By the time she reached the point concerning the "mutilation of watchband in my office," she was visibly shaking and shedding tears as she waved around a plastic bag containing a watch with one side of the watchband completely cut off. "This is a watch that my daughter gave to me," she said. "It is very special and someone came into my office one night and chopped off a little piece of the band after I had accidentally left it on my desk. Each time I forgot it in my office, someone came in and chopped off another piece."

Snowden was unable to say whether the watchband mutilator was the same person who broke into her office to change the margins on her computer. Nor was she able to explain why she kept leaving her watch overnight on her office desk after someone commenced to mutilate it.

I am really concerned about this person, Sam. It is obvious that these bizarre events have never actually happened. Clearly, the other members of the department didn't believe the charges, since they all voted to give Cecil another term as our department chair. But there is a question as to whether Snowden actually believed that these things have happened. If not, wouldn't you agree that she is simply an evil person? If so, don't you think that you have a moral obligation to provide her with appropriate medical attention? As it stands, do you think that she is fit to be a college professor? I look forward to the results of your investigation.

Chasing Whitey and Fighting Cultural Insensitivity

Dear Mr. Staples:

I want to talk to you about the recent speech you gave at UNCW (for the low price of $7,500) on the topic of cultural awareness and sensitivity. Before you came to speak, I had already heard about your book, entitled *Parallel Time: Growing up in Black and White*. I have read portions of that book that recount your experiences as a young black male having to deal with stereotypes at the hands of whites.

Examples of the oppression you reported in the book were mainly experienced in your youth. This included white women clutching their purses when you passed and couples walking to the other side of the street to avoid you. These were undoubtedly painful and traumatic experiences for you, and I understand why you explained them solely in terms of white racism. However, even more interesting than the experiences themselves was the way that you dealt with them as a young graduate student at the University of Chicago. The following passage from your book is illustrative:

> *I was walking west on 57th Street, after dark, coming home from the lake. The man and the woman walking toward me were laughing and talking but clammed up when they saw me. The man touched the woman's elbow, guiding her toward the curb. Normally, I'd have given way and begun to whistle, but not this time. This time I veered toward them and aimed myself so that they'd have to part to avoid walking into me . . . I suppressed the urge to scream in (the man's) face . . . A few steps beyond them I stopped and howled with laughter. I called this game Scatter the Pigeons.*
>
> *Fifty-seventh Street was too well lit for the game to be much fun; people didn't feel quite vulnerable enough . . . The block was long and lined with young trees that blocked out the streetlight and obscured the heads of people coming towards you.*
>
> *One night I stopped beneath the branches and came up on the other side, just as a couple was stepping from their car into their town house. The woman pulled her purse close with one hand and reached for her husband with the other. The two of them stood frozen as I bored down on them. I felt a surge of power: these people were mine; I could do with them as I wished. If I'd been younger, with less to lose, I'd have robbed them, and it would have been easy. All I'd have to do was stand silently before them until they surrendered their money. I thundered, "Good Evening!" into their bleached-out faces and cruised away laughing.*

Anyone reading that passage should recognize the absurdity of your conduct. They should also wonder why you would write a book in which you boast about such childish behavior and blame it on the racism of others. But I wonder whether you are aware that your conduct is likely to reinforce unfair stereotypes of black males.

After sharing that disturbing passage with some of my students, one of them pointed out the fact that, a) your conduct legally constituted assault, and b) your victims were chosen on the basis of their race. He stopped short of suggesting that you should be charged under hate crime statutes. But he did ask why UNCW paid you $7500 to speak on cultural diversity and sensitivity.

I couldn't answer that one.

Jesse Jackson, Jesus Christ, and Martin Luther King

===

Dear Fellow Death Penalty Opponent:

I just wanted to drop you an e-mail in reference to your apparent objections to my recent editorial in the local newspaper. I understand that although we are both opponents of the death penalty, you were pretty upset with my harsh criticisms of the current status of the abolitionist movement.

I recently learned of your objections to my editorial from a student who was enrolled in your freshman political science class. She seemed a little taken aback when you brought a copy of my editorial into your class and started waving it above your head (in front of about thirty freshmen), telling them that they should never listen to a Republican professor who both opposes the death penalty and supports George W. Bush.

As a PhD in political science, I am sure that you are aware that your candidate, Al Gore, is also a death penalty support-er. We can sort through the implications of that fact later. But, for the time being, I will ask you to confront me personally with your criticisms rather than denounce me by name in front of a captive audience of 30 teenagers.

Let me also add that your recent decision to approach me in the faculty men's room, asking why I had a problem with Jesse Jackson, wasn't really appropriate either. That really doesn't constitute a face-to-face dialogue. As you will recall, I was inside a bathroom stall listening to you yell at me from somewhere in the vicinity of the sink. All I really heard you say was that "all politicians lie (not just Rev. Jackson)" before someone flushed the toilet in an adjacent stall. Maybe we can get together for lunch and flush everything out, so to speak.

For the time being, let me just assure you that I wrote my editorial criticizing Jackson mainly because he compared the racist murderer Gary Graham to both Martin Luther King, Jr. and Jesus Christ. That's my problem with Jesse Jackson. And it doesn't make me a racist, as you seem to have hinted the other day in the men's room.

By the way, I have attached a copy of the editorial below. Maybe you can highlight the parts that you found offensive and mail them back to me. Then we can discuss it like adults. Or perhaps we can debate the issue in front of your freshman class. Enjoy the reading. I'll talk to you soon.

Texas Case Misrepresented
By Mike Adams

There aren't many Republicans from Texas who both support George W. Bush and oppose the death penalty. But I am one of them. However, the recent tactics of my fellow death penalty opponents almost make me embarrassed to speak out against the death penalty.

After the death sentence of Gary Graham was initially handed down, death penalty opponents hurled accusations of racism against the lone eyewitness to the shooting, until they found out that she was not Caucasian. Then they began to claim that she was just sadly mistaken.

Similar accusations were levied against Graham's trial attorney until they realized that he, too, was black. The attack on Graham's lawyer then began to focus on the fact that he didn't call any witnesses at the trial. Few of those critics seem to understand that this is commonplace in criminal trials. The reason for the general tendency of defense lawyers to refrain from presenting evidence of innocence is that there isn't any. In other words, most of the time the police get the right person.

In the Gary Graham murder trial there were even more compelling reasons for not calling all of the witnesses who claimed to have exculpatory evidence. In addition to their generally shoddy character, some of the witnesses that Graham's attorney "failed" to call would have offered testimony opening the door for rebuttal evidence concerning a week-long crime spree during which Gary Graham committed ten armed robberies, raped a woman at gunpoint, and shot two other people.

Also disappointing was the tactic employed by those who sought out former jurors from the Graham trial and presented them with information about those "other witnesses." Apparently, when told about the existence of unsworn, out-of-court statements by rejected defense witnesses, a couple of the former jurors said that they would have voted differently.

Would they have voted differently if they had heard more about Graham's ten other recent robberies? And what about the shootings and the rape? What if they had heard about his unsworn, out-of-court statements to bailiffs, indicating that he would kill all of the witnesses next time he committed an armed robbery?

Perhaps the most obscene part of the Graham fiasco was the role that various celebrities played in publicizing this execution. I sat back in amazement as movie stars and their spouses misstated crucial facts about the case on national television. This was all topped off by Jesse Jackson's comparison of Gary Graham to Jesus Christ and Martin Luther King, Jr. I know that many Christians who heard this comparison were outraged. I am certain that many true civil rights leaders were as well.

Any claims about the status of Gary Graham as a martyr should have been laid to rest when he called upon the black panthers to converge upon Huntsville with weapons in hand. When they did so, many law-abiding citizens of Huntsville were forced to stay home from work and remain inside of their homes for fear of their safety. Though there was no significant violence, it remains to been seen whether anyone will act upon Graham's appeal to respond "by any means necessary" in the aftermath of his execution.

While all of this was taking place, the Fifth Circuit Court of Appeals in New Orleans lifted an indefinite stay on the execution of a mentally retarded Texas inmate named John Paul Penry. Penry has an IQ of around 53 and was abused so badly that Texas had to institutionalize him for a period of six years.

I have argued for sparing the life of John Paul Penry on moral grounds without manufacturing false claims of factual innocence. Governor Bush recently informed me that he would not be intervening in this execution. I know that in the coming months, the media will attack Bush if he allows Penry to be executed.

I hope that those in the media who have just used the Graham execution as a political device against Bush will recall the 1992 presidential campaign. During that campaign, a young governor from the state of Arkansas was forced to choose between political life and human life when a severely mentally impaired man (who previously had a frontal lobotomy) was facing execution.

Clinton left New Hampshire to oversee that execution. After leaving part of his last meal untouched, the inmate said that he would come back for it later. Though unaware of what was happening, he lost his life. Clinton also lost the New Hampshire primary. Where were the black panthers? Where was Jesse Jackson? What has happened to the dignity of the abolitionist movement?

Smile!
You're on Councilwoman's Camera

Dear Chancellor Leutze:

I assume that by now you have read the Wednesday edition of the *Wilmington Star News*, featuring City Councilwoman Katherine Moore's latest run-in with the Wilmington Police Department. I am writing to you because, as you know, Ms. Moore is also a member of the UNC-Wilmington Board of Trustees. I know that you are also aware that she was recently accused of calling a police officer "white trash" after the officer gave her daughter a parking ticket in front of a local supermarket.

I addition to writing you about Ms. Moore's conduct, I am also spending the day reading the book Ms. Moore wrote in 1999 under a pseudonym. I am extremely disturbed by certain accusations she levies in the book against various members of our local government. She documents a variety of transgressions including, but not limited to, child molestation and bestiality. You will be receiving my review of this disturbing book some time in the next few days.

For the time being, I would like to know your thoughts about Ms. Moore's altercation with the police on Tuesday night. The incident started when an officer tried to ticket Councilwoman Moore's daughter, who had apparently been driving the wrong way down a one- way street. When the officer turned on his lights, Moore's daughter called her using her cell phone. When Moore arrived at the traffic stop, things got interesting. Their exchange (which was printed in the newspaper) follows:

> *COUNCILWOMAN MOORE:* And what was the problem?
> *OFFICER MILLER:* She is being stopped because she was in reverse in a one-way.
> *COUNCILWOMAN MOORE:* She is being stopped?
> *OFFICER MILLER:* She had her vehicle in reverse and was traveling the wrong way on this one-way street here.
> *COUNCILWOMAN MOORE:* She was backing up, right?
> *OFFICER MILLER:* Yes, sir, she was.
> *COUNCILWOMAN MOORE:* She can't back up?
> *OFFICER MILLER:* Not in the wrong direction.
> *COUNCILWOMAN MOORE:* … That other little piece of (inaudible) got away with it, but okay. You know exactly what you're doing, too. I'll be damned. That is why all we heard tonight was the Wilmington Police ain't doing nothing for crime. You ain't got time to do nothing for crime because all you can do is harass … Don't worry about it, Sweetie. Don't worry about it …We can afford to pay this little ticket, he can't. And I'm going to have something for (Police Chief) John Cease this evening … They can't stand us living like we live. I can't deal with prejudiced people

OFFICER MILLER: Just to let you know, I have a councilwoman's daughter here stopped and now she is behind me. She's impeding the flow of traffic. I am trying to deal with her daughter and she keeps getting in my face.

COUNCILWOMAN MOORE: Just as long as he didn't stop you in the dark where he could accost you.

OFFICER MILLER: I will get to you in just a second as soon as I'm done explaining the citation. OK? Ma'am, you need to step back from me until I'm done explaining the citation, please.

COUNCILWOMAN MOORE: Okay. That'll be fine. I just want to make sure you're not going to beat her up like *you all* normally do black people. I just want to make sure you are not going to beat her up.

It would seem from the above transcript that Ms. Moore's previous denial concerning her use of the phrase "white trash" is implausible given her comment to officer Miller (concerning his inability to afford a traffic ticket). It certainly looks like we have a racist on the UNCW Board of Trustees. It is also ironic that she was caught making racist remarks on one of the police patrol-car cameras that she had previously voted to purchase for the city as a means of reducing police abuse of minorities.

To make matters worse, Chancellor, the police have since released an audiotape of Moore accusing another officer of racism during a 1998 traffic stop. I have included portions of the transcript of that conversation below:

OFFICER NEDLEY: ... Do you have a license on you ma'am?

MS. MOORE: It's at the house. Can I go?

OFFICER NEDLEY: You do not have your license on you?

MS. MOORE: No. I put it in another pocketbook.

OFFICER NEDLEY: The reason I pulled you is because I was going 45, okay. I noticed that when you passed me and waved, I could not figure out why you were waving, and then you just took off, and then I paced you at 57 miles an hour.

MS. MOORE: I certainly was not going 57 when you stopped me.

OFFICER NEDLEY: No. Well ... when you noticed I was behind you, you slowed back down a little ways and then you pulled over ... What I'm going to do is issue you a citation for your speed ...

MS. MOORE: Okay. The gloves are off ... This man is lying. The gloves are off ... The police continue to stop me. I have a record where they were sitting in my yard with a blue light running. I am taking this to ...

OFFICER NEDLEY: A blue light running?

MS. MOORE: Oh, yes ... In my yard. They were sitting in my yard with the light running.

OFFICER NEDLEY: What are you talking about? ...

MS. MOORE: I am talking about what has happened since I have been on the city council ...

OFFICER NEDLEY: Ma'am, when you are speeding you have to go by the law.

MS. MOORE: I'm going to court against the whole damn department. I am tired of being harassed by ya'll. I'm getting sick and damn tired of it. You harass every black person in this town and more importantly you harass all the black elected officials.

OFFICER NEDLEY: Are you saying that I'm racist, ma'am?

MS. MOORE: Yes, sir.

OFFICER NEDLEY: Okay.

MS. MOORE: Yes, I'm saying that you harass every single-ya'll harass every black person in this town.

OFFICER NEDLEY: Who is ya'll.

MS. MOORE: The Wilmington Police Department ... (inaudible) ... come to my house all the time. Yes, I'm tired of it.

OFFICER NEDLEY: What? Somebody is watching your house?

OFFICER NEDLEY: You do not even know me to sit here and say that I am racist.

MS. MOORE: Well, I'll put it this way: If you're not, you're the first white on that force since (inaudible) Williamson that was not a racist. This is all I have to say.

OFFICER NEDLEY: Well, I understand ... You have a good day ma'am.

This is disturbing, Dr. Leutze. As you know, the city council just convened a special session to censure Ms. Moore for her behavior. I am hoping that you will see fit to ask for her resignation from the UNCW Board of Trustees. After all, we have been emphasizing cultural sensitivity and diversity for years at UNCW. Certainly, no white member of the Board of Trustees could use a term like "black trash" in public and get away with it. This problem really needs no further elaboration. Let me know what you plan to do.

Lizards in the Attic

Dear Chancellor Leutze,

I recently wrote you concerning the behavior of Katherine Moore, a member of the UNCW Board of Trustees. Despite numerous requests, she recently refused to step down from city council, saying that she would not allow a few minutes of anger to define her. Of course, similar arguments have been made by the likes of O.J. Simpson and Mike Tyson.

The argument that Ms. Moore should not be defined by a few minutes of anger is of no relevance to the question of her fitness to serve on the UNCW Board of Trustees. I am assuming that she spent more than a few minutes writing her 189-page book entitled *Under Oath: Memoirs of an Honest Politician.* Below, I have provided a few highlights from her book that will be followed by a couple of questions.

On page 30, Ms. Moore makes it clear that her

("There are many times that I fear for my life and the lives of my family members."), and then specific (When I went out to my new car, the right rear tire was slashed. As I got into the car, a helicopter circled so low over me that I could almost reach out and touch it.")

On page 147, she states, "After each council meeting, the city clerk follows me home and waits while I go into my house and check for intruders. I never go anywhere without my firearm. My son lives in Louisburg, N.C. Unmarked cars have accosted him many times on dark deserted roads . . ."

After pages of similar problems in Massachusetts, Moore states on page 171, "My friends and neighbors have become my stalkers" and "have become the eyes and ears for those who sought to destroy me."

The rest is redundant.

The proper way to evaluate Ms. Moore's fitness to serve on the UNCW Board of Trustees is by asking the following question: Does Ms. Moore a) believe the things she has written in her book? Or has she, b) intentionally fabricated her stories? If the answer is "a", Ms. Moore is mentally unqualified to sit on the Board of Trustees. If the answer is "b", she is morally unqualified to sit on the Board of Trustees. It might also be helpful to ask how, precisely, Ms. Moore's conduct at various traffic stops can be squared with UNCW's heavy emphasis on diversity and cultural sensitivity.

Until now, I have heard the administration respond to questions about this situation in two ways: first, by offering "no comment" and, second, by suggesting that there is no way to remove Ms. Moore from her position. Assuming the latter to be true, does this mean that the administration must, therefore, remain silent on this issue?

A number of students and faculty have expressed outrage over Ms. Moore's conduct. Nonetheless, most have kept a low profile. Some untenured professors have indicated that they will not speak out against Ms. Moore because of her role in the tenure and promotion decision process. In that sense, Ms. Moore's association with UNCW is already exerting a chilling effect on constitutionally protected free speech.

I sincerely hope that, above all of the other voices that she hears, Ms. Moore will listen to the voice of reason calling for her to resign from the UNCW Board of Trustees. I respectfully ask the administration to speak out on this issue if she should chose to do otherwise. When UNCW does speak out, it should do so in a manner which gives full assurance to the students and faculty at UNCW that they will in no way suffer from the abuses of power Ms. Moore has already displayed in public and on camera. I respectfully await your response.

POSTSCRIPT: The Chancellor did respond to my letter. He said that it would be inappropriate to comment on her qualifications since he had no role in appointing or removing people from the Board of Trustees. He then concluded his letter by saying that Ms. Moore had performed a "valuable" service to the university.

The Women's Resource Center

Dear Provost Cavanaugh:

I am writing you again to express my disappointment concerning the establishment of a new Women's Resource Center (WRC) here at UNCW. My concerns about the WRC are even greater than my concerns about the previously established African American Cultural Center. Obviously, blacks can be considered minorities on our campus on the basis of their numerical representation (I think they are only about six percent of the student population at UNCW). Women, on the other hand, comprise about sixty percent of the students on our campus. They don't seem to be oppressed in any way since they also outperform their male counterparts in the classroom.

Do you remember the first time I wrote to you to express my concerns about the WRC? I had just heard that a women's center was being proposed, and I contacted you to express my objections. At that time you called the rumor about a new WRC a "distorted version of the truth." You then told me that an "ad hoc committee" had been formed to conduct a survey of possible interest in a "women's leadership minor." I then requested a copy of the survey and its results.

A few weeks later you sent me a copy of that survey. Later, Dr. Janet Ellerby in the English Department provided me with a copy of the survey's results. The information I received clearly indicated that the rumors I heard weren't in the least bit "distorted." The survey was not about a "women's leadership minor." It was about a Women's Resource Center.

At first I thought that the "ad hoc committee" might have decided on its own to look into the idea of a Women's Resource Center without your knowledge or approval. However, I recently looked at your vita online and noticed that under your listing of "accomplishments" as provost, there was a line which read "Initiated and developed the first Women's Resource Center at UNCW."

I know that this "accomplishment" will pad your vita and impress campus feminists. I also know that it will look good as you advance in your career. But do the students really want the WRC? If you still have a copy of the survey, take a look at it again.

Perhaps the most notable portion of the survey is the absence of a question asking students whether they *want* a Women's Resource Center. Instead, students are simply asked what services they "would like to see offered in such a center." Of the thirty programs and services the students were asked about, only six were preferred by a majority of students polled (most respondents were women). Only one prospective service (self-defense classes) reached a two-thirds majority. Like many of the other services on the "survey," these classes are already offered on campus. Doesn't that seem strange to you? Did you design this survey?

I know that at least one campus feminist will get a big pay raise when she is appointed to direct the new WRC. But how can you justify that in the midst of a state budget crisis and talk of new tuition hikes? And, by the way, faculty members are still paying for their own parking passes. I think it now costs $172 per year just to come to work.

Oh well, I guess the money is always available for the really important things. Please write back with your thoughts. And remember to be honest and forthright at all times.

A Matter of Public Record

Dear Mr. White:

As you know, last November an officer in the UNCW police department asked me to stop by the station to discuss a matter involving former Faculty Senate President Lynne Snowden. When I arrived at the police station, the officer informed me that Snowden had reported to them that her office was being burglarized. She claimed that the burglar was spraying some form of poison in the office in an apparent act of "workplace terrorism." As you may know, Snowden has written a book on terrorism and teaches a course on the subject.

I was quite pleased with the professionalism of the officer who interviewed me in November. He immediately expressed the view that Snowden was in need of a psychiatrist. That was a relief to hear since she had named me as the person responsible for the "terrorism" of her office. As you already know, she also accused our department chair, Cecil Willis, of using his master keys to let me into her office to spray the mysterious toxins that she claimed were cutting off the circulation in her legs.

I found it particularly interesting that Snowden told the officer that her doctors were not able to find anything physically wrong with her. I was also interested to find that Snowden convinced an adjunct faculty member and a criminal justice major to come into her office to "swatch" her desk in order to preserve a sample of this mysterious poison gas. The officer also said that Snowden suspected that the mysterious toxin was tear gas.

I was also pleased that the officer said that he would try to get Snowden's accusations on tape. Before I left, he also indicated that he knew about her previous false claims of harassment against Willis.

Interestingly, the campus news bulletin announced later in the month that Cecil Willis was a candidate for the position of Associate Provost and Vice President for Academic Affairs at UNCW. As you know, after that announcement the police interviewed Snowden again. You also probably heard that she then altered her theory on the "workplace terrorism" charges. Specifically, she accused Willis of breaking into her office. She had apparently relegated me to the role of accessory.

After Christmas break I noticed that Snowden's ability to function in the workplace was diminished. On many occasions I saw her wearing slippers as she walked into class, dragging her left leg behind her. That tear gas must have been pretty strong to cut off the circulation in her left leg. However, I did wonder why it didn't affect the 80-pound Labrador retriever that she took into her office at night for personal protection. Of course, I also wondered what kind of education the students were getting in Snowden's classes.

By March of this year, I noticed that Snowden had stopped
going into her office altogether. She began using the computer in the main office and started advising students in the computer lab just down the hall. It was also becoming common
knowledge on campus that Snowden believed that terrorists
were after her. A colleague of mine saw her one evening
around six o'clock in the office hallway, using a towel to get
the mail out of her mailbox before dropping it into a plastic
bag. According to another colleague, she was afraid to touch
it until she had sanitized it in a microwave oven.

In early April, I was informed that the UNCW police had
met with the Dean of Arts and Sciences, Jo Ann Seiple, to discuss the results of a police investigation into Snowden's
charges. As you know, I had consented in January to a short
interview with the police. They declined to inform me of my
Miranda rights after telling me that they did not consider me
a criminal suspect. They also sent swatches from Snowden's
office to the State Bureau of Investigation in order to make
sure that no crime actually took place. The results were, of
course, negative. It seemed as if the police were meeting with
the dean to urge psychiatric intervention in the matter.

Next, I called the UNCW police in order to obtain transcripts of their interviews with Snowden. After none of my
three phone calls were returned, I had Willis call them to
ascertain the location of the transcript. They informed Willis
that you were in possession of all such transcripts. You will
recall that I then submitted a public records request to you for
those transcripts on April 9th. After sixteen days and no
response, I tried to contact you again.

I appreciated your response to my second message indicating that you had been out of town recently. I also appreciated
your promise to look into the matter to determine whether I
had a right to the transcripts under North Carolina law. After

a week elapsed without hearing your decision, I tried again to get an answer via e-mail. Finally, I set up an appointment to hand deliver another formal public records request prepared with the assistance of my attorney, Charlton Allen.

I understand why you ultimately denied that request. Giving me the information necessary to defend my reputation would have meant that the public would learn that the university's former Faculty Senate President (later the chair of the Faculty Senate budget committee) had gotten away with accusing colleagues of sexual harassment, burglary, and terrorism for many years with impunity.

Sacrificing my interest for the interests of the university was a bad idea, Mr. White. The university's refusal to deal with this dangerous faculty member shows just how morally depraved this institution has become. If Snowden really believes her bizarre allegations, she is *mentally* unfit to teach at the university. If, on the other hand, she does not believe the allegations, she is *morally* unfit to teach at the university. You simply cannot ignore this matter and hope that it will go away quietly. I promise that the general public will know the whole story in the end. If you are reading this chapter, they already do.

PART TWO

An "Out of the Closet" Conservative Speaks Out

The Campus Crusade
Against Christ

Although I was a liberal and an atheist when I began teaching at UNC-Wilmington, I was taken aback by the prevalence of anti-Christian sentiment, as well as by the degree of comfort professors felt in expressing it both inside and outside the classroom. Over the years, I have heard students complain about professors calling Christianity a "violent religion," or telling their students who believe the Bible that they have a "problem" because evolution is a "proven theory." Others boldly label Biblical objections to homosexuality as a form of "bigotry" or a "phobia," implying a need for either sensitivity training or psychotherapy.

While I have learned to question student accounts of what transpires in the classroom, I have seen enough of this sentiment firsthand to know that it cannot be dismissed. Indeed, anyone who visits our campus can see that some professors proudly adorn their office doors with emblems showing a "Darwin fish" swallowing a "Jesus fish" or bumper stickers saying, "Homophobia is a social disease." The messages are clear. Evolution is true. Christianity is false. Homosexuals are normal. People who believe Leviticus are sick.

Far more important than what goes on professors' doors is what goes on behind closed doors in university recruitment meetings. At my university, I have heard professors object to job candidates because they "seemed too religious" or they "seemed like too much of a family man." One professor had the audacity to criticize faith-based initiatives with the comment that "he didn't want his tax dollars going to the f—-ing church." That statement was uttered while he was having lunch with a job candidate.

The comments of individual professors are even less disturbing than the dominant themes emanating from the various programs and centers, which have been inspired by the broader "diversity" movement in academia. For example, the Women's Resource Center at UNC-Wilmington urges pregnant students to seek the counsel of Planned Parenthood, while systematically blocking the efforts of pro-life groups to make their counseling services available. The Women's Center at UNC-Chapel Hill uses university resources to organize political action campaigns to preserve the legality of partial birth abortion. Their mass political e-mails describe the phrase "partial-birth abortion" as an "inflammatory term invented by the right wing." Christians who object to abortion are either ignored or portrayed as dangerous extremists.

More recently, universities have hosted seminars intended to promote sensitivity to gays, lesbians, bisexuals, and transgendered persons. I recently attended one of those seminars at UNCW where two cross-dressers instructed the audience on ways to avoid offending people who routinely switch back and forth between being a man and a woman. One cross-dresser informed the audience that some of these people are not gay. He/she added that the heterosexual cross-dressers think they are better than the gay cross-dressers because "they're like the Catholics who think they're the only ones going to heaven." So much for offending the Catholics.

At UNC-Chapel Hill, a six-month study initiated by the provost concluded that an Office of Lesbian, Gay, Bisexual, Transgendered, and Queer-Identified (LGBTQ) Life and Study was needed. Furthermore, the need to tolerate and even "embrace the diversity" created by LGBTQ people was stressed. The study also described UNC-Chapel Hill as "behind the times" because students are not allowed to major in "queer studies."

The recent decision requiring incoming UNC freshmen to read a Muslim devotional entitled *Approaching the Qurán* comes as no surprise to those of us who have been paying attention to the diversity movement. After years of focusing on race, gender, and sexual orientation, the movement finally decided to become involved in religious matters by embracing Islam last September.

Christians should welcome this new prong of the diversity agenda by making their presence known on campus. Students, professors, and staff should begin to wear jewelry and T-shirts adorned with crosses. If the administration makes any disparaging remarks, they should be reminded of their commitment to cross-dressing. Wherever "gay friendly" rainbow stickers are found on professor's doors, "Christian friendly" stickers could be made and placed beside them.

Perhaps the different themes of the diversity movement could eventually be brought together with a lecture series on the lack of queer studies programs in Islamic nations. If those are well attended, maybe there could be whole courses on the status of the feminist movement in the Middle East. If the courses fill up, we could petition to have next year's freshmen read a book about the role of Christianity in the abolition of slavery.

For too long, Christians have been complaining bitterly about the current climate on college campuses. But getting angry at the patently absurd solves nothing. We must respond with both reason and ridicule, in proper balance. Only then will we lift the veil on dogmatism disguised as diversity.

UNC Feminists Abort Free Speech

When a new Women's Resource Center was established at my
university (UNC-Wilmington), I was concerned that it would
serve as more of a resource for feminist professors than for female
students. I also suspected that the Center would try to advance a
"pro-choice" agenda with little tolerance for the views of pro-life
advocates. Recently, those suspicions were confirmed.

During a recent visit to their Web page, I noticed that the
Women's Resource Center claimed a dedication to education
and advocacy on a variety of issues facing women of "all backgrounds, beliefs, and orientations." The Center also claimed
an interest in working with many community-based organizations and in maintaining "clear lines of communication"
between the students and "any organizations involved."

Nonetheless, when I clicked on the portion of the Web site
which provides links to community organizations, I noticed

that contact information for Planned Parenthood, a "pro-choice" organization, was posted — while contact information for Life Line, a "pro-life" center, was conspicuously absent.

Without hesitation, I contacted the site's manager with a simple request for the Center to add contact information for Life Line in close proximity to the contact information for Planned Parenthood. After being directed to Dr. Kathleen Berkeley, I repeated that request. Dr. Berkeley was one of the professors who pushed for the establishment of the Women's Resource Center. She was also placed in charge of the center until its first official director assumed her duties in July 2002. After a few days of deliberation, which included a meeting with the dean, Dr. Berkeley denied my request stating, "The addition of Life Line Pregnancy Center would duplicate information provided by Planned Parenthood."

Of course, there is no "non-duplication requirement" for organizations posting information on the Center's Web page. For example, two of the community organizations on their site offer rape crisis counseling. Certainly, no reasonable person could object to that kind of "duplication." Imagine, hypothetically, that someone wanted to build a second domestic violence shelter in town. Certainly, the Women's Center would not deny a request to post their contact information because they already had information on another such shelter.

Dr. Berkeley's supposed "non-duplication" standard is both non-existent and unworkable. It is also utterly inapplicable to the case at hand. The differences between Life Line and Planned Parenthood are far greater than their similarities. The decision to keep Life Line's information away from students is yet another silly episode which reveals the fundamental dishonesty of the university's so-called commitment to diversity. It is no accident that the university library has a copy of Planned Parenthood's response to Bernard Nathanson's

Silent Scream, although they do not have a copy of the *Silent Scream* itself. The university library also houses a book by Dr. Berkeley, which refers to the *Silent Scream* as "grisly sensationalism." It would appear that the university would rather have their students read reviews offered from one perspective than to have students look at the original and assume the risk that they might come up with a different opinion.

The problem with higher education today is not that people are unaware that the diversity movement is dishonest. The problem is that among those people with reasonable objections to the diversity agenda, there are too few willing to do something about it. Administrators at public universities simply have no right to take money from taxpayers and use it to advance their own political causes while systematically suppressing the views of their opponents.

I hope that everyone reading this article will "duplicate" my efforts to expand the marketplace of ideas at their local university. If your tax dollars are being used to support a one-sided view on the issue of abortion, respectfully ask for information on the other side to be included. If you are denied, take your case before the court of public opinion or, if necessary, a court of law. After all, the right to free speech is older than the "right to choose." And censorship is decidedly "anti-choice."

UPDATE:
My second request to Dr. Berkeley was ignored. In July, Dr. Elizabeth Ervin became the permanent director of the Women's Resource Center. While she has characterized Dr. Berkeley's reasoning as "a rather lame justification," she agrees with her conclusion. Ervin justifies Life Line's exclusion on the grounds that it is "overtly religious."

Welcome To UNC-San Francisco

On October 11, 2002, the Chancellor of UNC-Wilmington sent a memo to all university faculty and staff, notifying them that the Executive Cabinet had approved Project B-GLAD which is designed to foster a more open and "affirming" campus environment for gay, lesbian, bisexual, and transgendered students, faculty, and staff. The memo boasted that the program's training sessions have produced over 100 individuals who are now willing to serve as allies for this constituent of our community. The memo also posited recognition of *National Coming Out Day* as its principal purpose.

I am pleased that the Chancellor's memo employed such terms as "allies" and "constituent(s)." Perhaps this is some indication that the administration is aware that there is currently a cultural war taking place on our college campuses. Perhaps this is also an admission that the diversity agenda is, at its core, a political movement.

Last year, I had the opportunity to attend a seminar at UNCW on the legal rights of transgendered persons. The seminar, which was run by a Charlotte attorney, featured two transgendered panelists. The analysis of their job-related legal difficulties was somewhat terse as one panelist admitted that she was not fired after changing gender. It seems that she, formerly he, simply quit. She admitted that her resignation posed difficulties for a possible lawsuit for wrongful termination. I assume that she knew what she was talking about as she was employed as a law enforcement officer when she was still a he.

The other panelist was employed at Radio Shack before being terminated for disrupting the workplace. She, once a he, admitted to these disruptions by declaring that she "can be a real b**ch when people get sh**ty" with her." These disruptions were justified in her view because people gave her an "attitude" about the sex change. She had no lawsuit pending for obvious reasons.

Having disposed of the complex legal issues involved in the cases of these two transgendered persons, the attorney then moved on to answer more serious questions, such as "which bathroom does a transgendered person use?" I was pleased to hear the attorney say that North Carolina does not have a specific law keeping men from using the women's restroom and vice versa. The next time I have too many cups of coffee before class I'll just bolt into the women's restroom, brush the co-eds aside, and make myself right at home. I think we all learned something about our legal rights that day, and I know that we are a better university as a result.

After answering legal questions, the attorney then took some time to announce her candidacy as a Democrat for a judicial opening in Charlotte. She also informed the audience that her principal reason for running was to lend support to the gay agenda from behind the bench. I am sure that this kind of campaigning adds to the perception that the university has become politically slanted despite all the emphasis on "diversity."

The issues I am raising are not limited to the Wilmington campus. Recently, the administration at UNC Chapel Hill encouraged a study, which has produced a recommendation for a Lesbian, Gay, Bisexual, Transgendered, and Queer-Identified Persons (LGBTQ) Life and Study Center. The study, initiated by the provost, also contained recommendations for a new "Queer Studies" major. It was suggested that the UNC system is "behind the times" when compared to universities in California. On a recent visit to the San Francisco State University Web site, I found one such major which included courses, such as "Queer Art History," "Homophobia and Coming Out," "Research in Sexual Identity," and "Field Service in Human Sexuality Studies."

In September of 2000, our university sponsored a "gay Christian" speaker who argued that homosexuality was compatible with the Bible. The speaker also ridiculed the idea of therapy designed to rid people of their homosexual tendencies. While arguing that homosexuality is not a disease, university gay activists regularly assert that *opposition* to homosexuality is a disease. Many post stickers on their office doors making that very assertion. To boldly label a person's constitutionally protected religious beliefs as "homophobia" is simply arrogant. It is certainly not a sign of sensitivity. Nor is it a sign of intellectual enlightenment.

Last summer when the university announced its first gay scholarship, officials made it clear that it was funded with private money. That emphasis demonstrates the university's awareness that the agenda it is pushing is one that the taxpayers do not support. However, there is much that the public does not know about the extent of the university's involvement in this agenda. The constitutionally protected speech in this article is designed to change that. If the university cannot defend itself in the court of public opinion, then it is change, rather than secrecy, that is needed. And the change that is needed does not come in the form of the vast majority relinquishing its values for the sake of the radical minority.

I hope that those who read this article will respect my First Amendment rights, as well as the rights I am guaranteed under state and federal copyright laws. The last time I dared to criticize gay activists at the university, my article ("The Campus Crusade Against Christ") was republished without my consent on a gay Web site operated by a university employee. After I attached my private e-mail address to the article, the employee replaced it with my university e-mail address. I well expected to receive criticism characterizing me as a "bigot" and a "fascist" from the "open-minded" proponents of the diversity movement. But I expected to avoid receiving these messages at my place of employment. Are my expectations reasonable, or am I in need of sensitivity training? I will leave it to the taxpayers to decide.

With hundreds of millions of dollars in state deficits, many of us would "B-GLAD" if the university would stop funding this nonsense.

The Cost of Diversity

While I was sitting at my computer the other day, I heard a strange dripping sound coming from the office next door. When I looked inside my colleague's office, I noticed that a trash can was catching the rain, which was leaking through his office roof. A few weeks ago, the classroom next door to mine had water leaking through four holes in its roof. While the professor was lecturing through the rainstorm, some students' view of the chalkboard was blocked by four trash cans perched on desk tables to keep water from splashing on their notebooks. Recently, I heard several students complain that they couldn't print out their assignments because the computer room was out of paper. Faculty members, who haven't had a pay raise in two years, have recently seen their health insurance increase. Faculty members also pay $172 per year to park at work.

While the university cannot seem to find the money to deal with some of these pressing issues, they always seem to find funding for the so-called diversity agenda. In fact, just a few days ago, the chancellor disseminated a report from a diversity task force that hints that diversity funding may soon increase dramatically. Listed among the reports' recommendations are new racial sensitivity training sessions for faculty. The report recommends that these sessions become a part of faculty performance evaluations. This is unsurprising given the university's recent funding of project B-GLAD, which includes sensitivity training sessions dealing with lesbian, gay, bisexual, and transgendered persons' issues.

The report also recommends a new "Associate Provost of Diversity" administrative position. This recommendation alone may cost the taxpayers six-digits per year if it is implemented. It should be noted that our university already has an "Office of Campus Diversity" with a director and a full-time staff. In addition to its support for project B-GLAD, the diversity office has sponsored some exciting events including a "gay Christian" speaker and a gay students' public reading of six papers written for his English class. The papers were about his "coming out" experience.

The diversity crowd also managed to get a black journalist to speak at UNCW for the low price of $7,500. Apparently, they were undeterred by the fact that he had published a book in which he boasted about chasing white people down the streets of Chicago for sport while he was in graduate school. In his book he did express regret, not for chasing white people, but, instead, for declining to rob them in the process. That was a bargain compared to the $12,000 spent on a speaker who referred to the Los Angeles riots—where Reginald Denny was dragged out of his truck and nearly beaten to death—as a "display of justified social rage." He claimed that it really wasn't a race riot.

The new diversity report's emphasis on the racial component of its agenda may well be in response to recent tension between two factions within the movement. One faction believes that the diversity agenda should focus on race while another thinks it should focus on sexual orientation. Statistics in the report indicate that, in addition to creating division within the movement, diversity funding has done little to increase minority enrollment. Of course, the administrative solution is to spend more money on diversity. Interestingly, one of the authors of the diversity report once wrote a book entitled "Wise Moves in Hard Times."

When I first began teaching at UNCW in 1993, I predicted much of what is happening now. When the university first entertained the idea of an African American Center, I predicted that Women's centers and Gay and Lesbian centers would eventually become a reality in the UNC system. The former prediction is already a reality, and the latter is in the planning stages.

Citizens should be concerned about these centers. While they are ostensibly created in the name of diversity, they are anything but diverse. For example, our Women's Center refuses to allow a local crisis pregnancy center to post contact information on its Web page next to Planned Parenthood because the CPC is "overtly religious." Hypocritically (and perhaps unconstitutionally?), the university provides links to a gay Web site which advertises churches and other "spiritual centers." One church's motto is "whatever you believe, we embrace you." One can also use this link to access reviews of books such as "The Oral Majority" and "The Ten Rules of Anal Sex."

Of course, one doesn't have to click on a link to get religious information from the UNCW Web site. Their "Project B-Glad" folder has plenty of religious references. In a list of 168 diverse books and articles on homosexuality (168 of which favor homosexuality), there are plenty of books about religion. Just to save some time, I'll list some representative entries; 1) *We Were Baptized Too: Claiming God's Grace for Lesbians and Gays* 2) *Wrestling With the Angel: Faith and Religion in the Lives of Gay Men,* 3) *Unrepentant, Self-Affirming, and Practicing: Lesbian, Gay, and Bisexual People Within Organized Religion,* 4) *Celebrations: Lesbians, Gays, and Bisexuals in the Church,* and 5) *The Truth Shall Set You Free: A Memoir on a Family's Passage from Fundamentalism.*

In the sake of fairness, not all of these titles are so explicit and adult. There are special readings on the university's Web site which are geared towards the youth. Again, here are some representative entries: 1) *Passages of Pride: Lesbian and Gay Youth Come of Age,* 2) *Helping Gay and Lesbian Youth: New Policies, New Programs, and New Practice,* 3) *Children of Horizons: How Gay and Lesbian Teens are Leading a New Way Out of the Closet,* 4) *Writings by Gay and Lesbian Youth,* and 5) *Understanding Sexual Identity: A Book for Gay Teens and Their Friends.*

Given that UNCW now has separate black faculty meetings, separate women's faculty meetings, and separate lunch meetings for black faculty and staff, some are beginning to question whether diversity proponents know where they are going with their heavily funded agenda. Many, like myself, fear that their vision of "progress" will soon include separate water fountains.

Reasonable people understand that when an idea fails consistently that it just might be wrong. But when we deal with diversity proponents, we are dealing with people who are at war with the very concepts of right and wrong. We are also dealing with people whose financial and political interests rely heavily on the success of the diversity movement. Indeed, if the diversity nightmare ever ends, it will not be the result of some sudden realization among college administrators that it is expensive, hypocritical, and divisive. It will only end when ordinary Americans realize that they can no longer afford to be silent.

God and Man at Carolina
(With Charlton Allen)

Christians and non-Christians alike were shocked when it was recently revealed that InterVarsity Christian Fellowship (IVCF), a student group at the University of North Carolina at Chapel Hill, had been threatened with de-recognition unless it allowed non-Christian students to serve as group officers.

Loss of university recognition for student groups is not a mere technicality. It denies these groups, among other things, the use of university facilities and access to university funding. Simply stated, it effectively bans such groups from campus altogether. After this story was broken by the Foundation for Individual Rights in Education (FIRE), the university rescinded its threat of de-recognition of IVCF in the midst of a national public relations firestorm.

Since the incident with IVCF, both of us have received several calls and e-mails concerning the incident. Most have posed a rather simple question: Is it really possible for college administrators to be so uneducated in the basics of civics that they would fail to recognize that the First Amendment to the United States Constitution trumps their school's diversity policies? Others marveled that the UNC administration had decided that Christian groups could exist on campus only if they would abandon their core religious beliefs and allow non-Christians to become leaders and members.

We immediately suspected that the incident at Chapel Hill was not an anomaly, but rather a function of the general animus towards Christians that exists on so many of our college campuses. After an article in the UNC student newspaper reported that a number of other organizations had also received letters threatening de-recognition, we decided that further examination was imperative. We initiated a public records request, pursuant to North Carolina law, demanding that UNC-Chapel Hill disclose all such correspondence. Given the rather large number of student organizations (481, to be exact), we wondered whether all groups had been carefully scrutinized or whether certain organizations were targeted.

Following our request, the university disclosed seventeen letters written by Assistant Director for Student Activities and Organizations Jonathan E. Curtis on December 10, 2002. In these letters, the following organizations were threatened with revocation of university recognition:

Music Makers Christian Fellowship, for stating that members of the servant team "are expected to model an appropriate Christian character to the rest of Music Makers."

Young Life, for referring to its membership as "a community of adult Christians."

The Lutheran Campus Ministry, for referring to its members as "a Christian community" and for requiring baptism as criteria for leadership in the organization.

The Episcopal Campus Ministry, for limiting its membership to "all Episcopal students attending UNC-CH, together with all those students from other Christian communions who chose to take the Chapel of the Cross and EMC as their parochial center."

Chi Alpha Omega Christian Fraternity, for limiting its membership to Christian males.

Chi Alpha Christian Fraternity, for requiring group leaders to commit to the goal of "discovering together what it means to have a relationship with Jesus Christ as the forgiver, healer and leader of [their] lives."

Alpha Epsilon Pi Fraternity, for limiting its membership to "any male student . . . who . . . believes in God." (No secular single-sex Greek societies at Carolina were threatened with de-recognition.)

Campus Crossroads, for requiring that "Leadership positions ... must be held by those professing Jesus Christ as their Savior and Lord."

Brotherhood in Christ, for limiting its membership to males.

The Bahá'ís of UNC-CH, for limiting their membership to those who believe in God.

The Native American Law Student Association, unless they allowed full participation "without regard to race."

The UNC-CH chapter of AISES (the American Indian Science and Engineering Society), because its members must be Native American unless granted "Special Membership."

IVCF was the only organization to which multiple letters were sent. In three separate letters, it was threatened with de-recognition for requiring its officers to subscribe to the Christian doctrine. Additionally, UNC-CH Habitat for Humanity and Phi Beta Kappa received letters concerning potential membership limitations unrelated to belief in God or in Christianity. These groups, however, were threatened with a mere suspension, not revocation.

The university has yet to comply with our demand for the release of similar correspondence from prior years. We suspect that if they do, the pattern will be the same, showing more examples of the University of North Carolina at Chapel Hill's abuse of the ministerial recognition process as a means to advance its own agenda unconstitutionally. The patent absurdity of the university's demands on these groups is compounded by the fact that they were all written under the guise of "diversity."

Regardless of whether these letters are a function of malice or sheer tomfoolery, the remedy is clear. Indeed, this is not a situation likely to provoke a war between our Constitution and common sense. Both compel the same result.

Nonetheless, to date the only organization that has challenged this intimidating practice is IVCF. Their success in forcing UNC-Chapel Hill Chancellor James Moeser to rescind the university's threat of de-recognition should serve as an inspiration to the other organizations involved, and to others who are able and willing to take up their cause.

Last summer, many academics were outraged when the North Carolina legislature drafted an amendment that they interpreted as an effort to prevent the teaching of the Koran in the UNC system. Their cries for academic freedom were heard across the state. But where are their voices now? What has happened to the principles once held in common by Christians and non-Christians alike? What has happened to the light of liberty that once shone so brightly upon the hill?

Sense-orship and Sensibility

Last night as I was walking into the university cafeteria to grab a sandwich, something unusual caught my attention. A large sign resting on an easel said "P**sies Unite for the 'Vagina Monologues,' February 16th... sponsored by the Women's Resource Center." For those of you who don't know, *The Vagina Monologues* is a feminist play performed annually on many college campuses across the nation. One of the play's highlights involves the simultaneous chanting of the word "vagina" by a bunch of young feminists holding hands and seeking unity.

After reading the sign promoting *The Vagina Monologues*, a young co-ed asked me where she could go to complain about the location of the offensive advertisement. It wasn't long before she found a university employee who assured her that she wasn't the first person to take offense. Apparently, a woman visiting campus had noticed the sign earlier with her four-year-old child. All complains were channeled to the director of the UNC-Wilmington Women's Resource Center (WRC).

I was not among those who complained to the WRC. I didn't want to be accused of censorship by University Leftists who seldom understand that freedom of speech is a safeguard to protect individual speech from governmental suppression. They often see it instead as a mechanism designed to protect governmental speech from taxpayer criticism.

I also knew that it was useless to complain directly to the person who actually put the sign there in the first place. Instead, I simply pondered the seemingly boundless hypocrisy and absurdity that characterizes the campus diversity movement. Various diversity centers, including campus women's centers, account for a large portion of the problem.

Just last month, I invited the director of the WRC to a roundtable discussion on abortion sponsored by the student pro-life group (I serve as the group's advisor). In fairness, I invited two other campus feminists as well as three pro-life advocates. The WRC director declined because I was conducting the discussion in conjunction with a showing of Bernard Nathanson's *Silent Scream* and Planned Parenthood's critique of the film. Although I was simply trying to be fair and balanced, she thought that Nathanson's film was "too inflammatory." Remember that this is the same person who was responsible for *The Vagina Monologues* and the call for all "p**sies" to unite.

Interestingly, the other feminist who wrote to decline my invitation to the roundtable discussion said that she didn't want to discuss abortion in public because the topic was "too personal." After telling her I respected her decision, I later discovered that she had published a 200-page memoir dedicated largely to the topic of abortion. The book, which also detailed her first sexual encounter in graphic terms, was reviewed by her fifth husband, dedicated to all of her children, and assigned to her "women in literature" students. But she wouldn't talk about abortion at my roundtable discussion. It was "too personal."

The third feminist I invited to the roundtable simply declined to respond. She had already opined (in a book on the feminist movement) that the *Silent Scream* was merely "grisly sensationalism." In other words, it was so obviously offensive that my invitation was deemed unworthy of a response.

Our chancellor has also employed the same tactic of ignoring requests for balanced presentation of ideas. After discovering 16 "recommended readings" on the Project B-Glad portion of our university Web site, all dealing with the relationship between "spirituality" and homosexuality, I noticed that they all shared the same view. Specifically, they presented homosexuality in a positive light and asserted compatibility between homosexuality and various religions such as Judaism and Christianity. I then submitted a list of eight books presenting a different view (by authors, such as James Dobson and Peter Kreeft) for posting on the university Web site. The chancellor simply ignored the request. Perhaps the fundamentalist readings were deemed too "offensive." I'll never know because he refuses to explain his decision.

It seems that the harder I try to initiate dialogue with the proponents of the so-called diversity movement, the more I realize that they are wholly uninterested in presenting diverse positions on any given subject. When they are confronted with ideas they don't like, they pretend to be easily offended. When they are expressing their own views, they are caustic and abrasive.

They call it diversity. I call it intellectual dishonesty.

Gay Pride and Prejudice

Some time ago, I came across an Internet advertisement promoting the 2003 North Carolina Unity Conference. This gathering of Lesbian, Gay, Bisexual, Transgendered, and Queer Identified (LGBTQ) persons and their "allies," took place on the campus of UNC-Chapel Hill. The conference, presented by a UNC student organization (the Gay, Lesbian, Bisexual, Transgendered-Straight Alliance), claimed to welcome people of all ages, races, genders, backgrounds, and "sexualities."

Despite the initial appearance of inclusion, another portion of the advertisement stated that the conference "strive(s) to be as inclusive as possible by limiting registration only to members or allies of the LGBTQ movement." This concept of discriminating in order to be "diverse" or "inclusive" defies logic in the eyes of most Americans. But it is rarely challenged at American universities.

In addition to the logical problems inherent in this restriction, there are also some practical difficulties. For example, how will conference organizers identify people who "look gay" during the registration process? If someone who doesn't "look gay" tries to enter, how will organizers know whether they are an "ally" of the gay movement? Will they fill out a survey? Or do they already have I.D. cards and special documents they can produce for prompt inspection? Perhaps the "Project B-Glad Ally" stickers that my university gives to those who complete gay sensitivity training sessions could be sewn on to people's garments for purposes of identification.

While many see the campus gay political movement as a source of humor, there is nothing funny about the way various campus religious groups are being treated at UNC Chapel Hill. Recently, national media attention focused on a threat to effectively ban Inter-Varsity Christian Fellowship (IVCF) from campus, because it requires that its officers subscribe to Christian doctrine. The controversy was sparked after a threatening letter from the administration demanded that the group alter its constitution in the name of "diversity."

After IVCF challenged the university, the chancellor rescinded the threat. However, one organizer of the so-called "Unity Conference" is now threatening to organize a "network" of alumni to withhold donations from UNC-CH unless the chancellor reinstates the threat against IVCF. Specifically, he criticizes the student group for adhering to "archaic notions of 'freedom of expression'" and "Levitican ridiculousness." All this because IVCF requires their officers to subscribe to Christian doctrine. Apparently, some gay activists are not content with removing orthodox Christians from college campuses. They also want to remove specific clauses from the Bill of Rights and entire books from the Old Testament.

Gay activists at UNC Chapel Hill should not be discouraged by their recent "defeat" at the hands of IVCF. Some members of the student government are still trying to withhold funding from the group. Additionally, a number of other student organizations are still threatened with revocation of university recognition because of their religious beliefs. Some examples of groups threatened last semester by the UNC administration follow: Music Makers Christian Fellowship, Young Life, Lutheran Campus Ministry, Episcopal Campus Ministry, Chi Alpha Omega Christian Fraternity, Chi Alpha Christian Fraternity, Alpha Epsilon Pi Fraternity, Campus Crossroads, and the Bahá'ís of UNC-CH.

Given the university's willingness to allow a gay student group to discriminate on campus at the "Unity Conference," many wonder why the numerous threats of de-recognition (directed overwhelmingly towards Christian groups) have not been rescinded. The answer is simple. Gay activists are fighting to keep them in place while Christians remain silent.

Presently, administrators are considering a proposal to develop a new LGBTQ Life and Study Center at UNC Chapel Hill. The Center's ostensible purpose is to provide a "safe zone" for Lesbians, Gays, Bisexuals, Transgendered, and Queer-Identified persons. But many who are not their "allies" are beginning to wonder where they can go to express deeply held beliefs not sanctioned by UNC administrators.

Clearly, gay activists are being granted more and more power by the administration as a result of their persistent claims of powerlessness. And the more they express their pride, the more they reveal their prejudice.

The Rap on Diversity

There have been several times over the last few years when I thought that the diversity movement at my university had reached its peak in terms of absurdity. However, I recently realized that the movement has reached a new level of lunacy even I could not have foreseen. This realization came as I was driving by the university and saw an advertisement for an upcoming university-sponsored concert featuring the rapper Ludacris.

For those who don't already know, Ludacris was recently dropped from an endorsement deal with Pepsi Cola as a result of negative publicity generated by the anchor of the Fox News program, *The O'Reilly Factor*. Bill O'Reilly seemed to have little trouble convincing the public that Ludacris was an undesirable Pepsi spokesperson, given his penchant for writing songs about "n**gas," "b**ches," and "hos."

After making a few phone calls, I found out that the UNCW Ludacris concert was being funded by $60,000 in student fees that was being matched by $60,000 in funding from the university. In other words, $120,000, which could have funded ten four-year full scholarships for minority students, would be spent in a few hours by funding live renditions of songs such as "Move B**ch" and "Get the F**k Back (or Luda Make Your Skull Crack)."

I raise the issue of minority scholarships because the university supported the idea of bringing in Ludacris, because it was believed that the rapper would help promote "diversity" at UNCW. The university has long been concerned about the fact that less than ten percent of its student population is black. In fact, the highest proportion of black students in UNCW history is only six percent. Now that the Office of Campus Diversity has spent its first million dollars, the proportion of black students is four percent.

Fortunately, every member of the so-called diversity movement is not embracing the appearance of Ludacris at UNCW. Recently, the director of the UNCW Women's Resource Center (WRC) indicated that most likely there would be a protest because of the rapper's misogynistic lyrics. However, some are not taking the threat of a WRC protest seriously due to their recent decision to sponsor *The Vagina Monologues*, which they advertised on campus with signs saying "P**sies Unite...for *The Vagina Monologues*." Apparently, the WRC objects to references to women as "b**ches" and "hos." They prefer the term "p**sies."

To make matters even worse, the university recently banned the playing of the "Cotton Eyed Joe" at university basketball games. After a modern version of the song had been playing at the games for three years, an African American member of the UNCW Board of Trustees demanded the song's removal from the play list at all university athletic functions. This was based on a false claim that the song contained references to the ownership of a black man. In reality, the version played at the games was a modern rendition that deleted the offensive references. Of course, reality is less important than "perceptions" and "feelings" in the eyes of diversity proponents.

Many observers following these recent free speech controversies are wondering why the university would sponsor the rapper Ludacris while banning the "Cotton Eyed Joe." When asked to explain the contradiction, the co-chair of the university's Diversity Task Force said she supported the banning of "Cotton Eyed Joe", even though she had never read the lyrics of the song. She called the song she had never heard both "offensive" and "disturbing." She did not object to the Ludacris concert, however. In fact, she said she "respected" the rap artist. When asked to justify the banning of one and not the other, she said that the issue was "too complex to explain."

Actually, the chaos that is currently prevailing on our college campuses is very easy to explain. Our constant emphasis on "diversity" has led to a prevailing campus philosophy of moral relativism that claims to consider all ideas to be equally valid. The UNCW Dean of Students recently articulated that philosophy when he was asked why the university was facilitating, rather than blocking, the appearance of Ludacris. He responded by saying that, "We don't want to be in the business of imparting values of right and wrong" to our students.

In reality, university administrators do promote diversity as a value that they consider to be "right." And the inherent contradiction in dubbing moral relativism as an absolute truth seems lost upon them all. That is why the university experience itself has become rife with hypocrisy and contradiction.

Never before has higher education been so truly ludicrous.

My New Affirmative Action Grading Policy

Dear UNC-Wilmington Students:

For years, my well-known opposition to affirmative action has been a source of great controversy across our campus, particularly among UNCW faculty. Many have assumed that my position on this topic has been a function of personal prejudice or "insensitivity" to the needs of various "disenfranchised" groups on campus and in society in general. In reality, my opposition to affirmative action has been based on personal experience.

When I first applied for a job as a university professor, a well-meaning department chair at Memphis State University (now the University of Memphis) told me that I had no chance of getting a job in his department because the only other finalist for the position was a black male. When I took a job at UNCW a month later, I hoped that I had found an environment devoid of such blatant racial discrimination. Unfortunately, my experiences here have proven otherwise. It is my constitutionally protected opinion that I have experienced direct pressure from the administration to engage in both racial and gender discrimination as a member of various university search committees.

Furthermore, I have seen examples of salary discrimination based on affirmative action. For example, one department at UNCW hired a black female as an assistant professor in 1999 before she had finalized her dissertation. Despite her inexperience, she was paid more than two tenured white male associate professors in her department who had, of course, finished their dissertations. One had been teaching at UNCW for five years, the other for seven years.

Despite all of this, I have decided to abandon my longstanding opposition to affirmative action after listening to the oral arguments in the recent US Supreme Court case challenging admissions policies at the University of Michigan. While listening to these recorded arguments, I learned that public universities have a "compelling interest in diversity" which trumps simplistic notions of reverse discrimination. Now, because my views have changed, I am forced to alter my classroom grading policies.

Students in my classes will continue to have their final grades based principally on test performance. Students will also continue to have a portion of their grade determined by class participation and/or a final paper, depending on the class in which they are enrolled (please consult your course syllabus if you are one of my students).

After I compute final averages, I will then implement the new aspect of the grading process that is modeled after existing affirmative action policies at the university. Specifically, I will be computing a class average that I will then compare to the individual performance of all white males enrolled in my classes. All white males who exceed the class average will have points deducted and added to the final averages of women and minorities. A student need not have ever engaged in discrimination in order to have points deducted. Nor must a student have ever been a victim of discrimination in order to receive additional points.

I expect that my new policy will be well received by some, and poorly received by others. For those in the latter category, please contact Human Resources for further elaboration on the concept of affirmative action. You may also contact the Office of Campus Diversity for additional guidance.

I understand that many of you may consider my new position to be unprincipled. Please understand, however, that the university has long abandoned antiquated principles of "fairness" in favor of identity politics. Also understand that my job as a university professor is to prepare you for the real world.

After all, no one promised that life would always be fair.

The Dini-Gration of Darwinism

Texas Tech University biology professor, Michael Dini, recently came under fire for refusing to write letters of recommendation for students unable to "truthfully and forthrightly affirm a scientific answer" to the following question: "How do you think the human species originated?"

For asking this question, Professor Dini was accused of engaging in overt religious discrimination. As a result, a legal complaint was filed against Dini by the Liberty Legal Institute. Supporters of the complaint feared that consequences of the widespread adoption of Dini's requirement would include a virtual ban of Christians from the practice of medicine and other related fields.

In an effort to defend his criteria for recommendation, Dini claimed that medicine was first rooted in the practice of magic. Dini said that religion then became the basis of medicine until it was replaced by science. After positing biology as the science most important to the study of medicine, he also posited evolution as the "central, unifying principle of biology," which includes both micro- and macroevolution and, that applies to all species.

In addition to claiming that someone who rejects the most important theory in biology cannot properly practice medicine, Dini suggested that physicians who ignore or neglect Darwinism are prone to making bad clinical decisions. He cautioned that a physician who ignores data concerning the scientific origins of the species couldn't expect to remain a physician for long.

He then rhetorically asked the following question: "If modern medicine is based on the method of science, then how can someone who denies the theory of evolution—the very pinnacle of modern biological science—ask to be recommended into a scientific profession by a professional scientist?"

In an apparent preemptive strike against those who would expose the weaknesses of macro-evolution, Dini claimed that "one could validly refer to the 'fact' of human evolution, even if all of the details are not yet known." Finally, he cautioned that a good scientist "would never throw out data that do not conform to their expectations or beliefs."

The legal aspect of this controversy ended with Dini finally deciding to change his recommendation requirements. But that doesn't mean that it's time for Christians to declare victory and move on. In fact, Christians should be demanding that Dini's question be asked more often in the court of public opinion. If it is, the scientific community will eventually be indicted for its persistent failure to address this very question in scientific terms.

Christians reading this article are already familiar with the creation stories found in the initial chapters of Genesis and the

Gospel of John. But the story proffered by evolutionists to explain the origin of the species receives too little attention and scrutiny. In his two most recent books on evolution, Phillip Johnson gives an account of the evolutionists' story of the origin of the human species that is similar to the one below:

In the beginning there was the unholy trinity of the particles, the unthinking and unfeeling laws of physics, and chance. Together, they accidentally made the amino acids that later began to live and to breathe. Then the living, breathing entities began to imagine. And they imagined God. But then they discovered science and then science produced Darwin. Later, Darwin discovered evolution and the scientists discarded God.

Darwinists who claim to be scientists are certainly entitled to hold this view of the origin of the species. But that doesn't mean that their view is, therefore, scientific. They must be held to scientific standards, requiring proof as long as they insist on asking students to recite these verses as a rite of passage into their "scientific" discipline.

It, therefore, follows that the appropriate way to handle professors like Michael Dini is not to sue them but, instead, to demand that they provide specific proof of their assertion that the origin of all species can be traced to primordial soup. In other words, we should pose Dr. Dini's question to all evolutionists. And we should do so in an open public forum whenever the opportunity presents itself.

Recently, I asked Dr. Dini for that proof. He didn't respond.

Dini's silence, as well as the silence of other evolutionists, speaks volumes about the current status of the discipline of biology. It is worth us asking whether the study of biology has been hampered by the widespread and uncritical acceptance of Darwinian principles. To some observers, its study has largely become a hollow exercise whereby atheists teach other atheists to blindly follow Darwin without asking any difficult questions. At least that seems to be the way things have evolved.

War and Peaceniks

A couple of weeks ago, I walked into my office and saw that someone had placed a poster on my desk that advertised a "walk out" in protest of Bush's war on terrorism. Unlike the walkouts of the sixties that were organized by students, this event was organized by a number of UNC-Wilmington professors and staff members, some of whom are avowed socialists.

The poster reflected all of the usual tactfulness and refinement of the University Left. Beside a picture of President Bush with the word "bully" printed across his forehead, there was a picture of Lady Liberty shoving a sword up the rectum of a dove. And, of course, no anti-war poster would be complete without desecrating the American flag. This particular poster did so by portraying the stripes of Old Glory in the form of air pollution trailing a squadron of B1 bombers.

When these posters were placed all over campus, a number

of students were predictably offended. In fact, many had family members fighting in the conflict. I was shocked to find that the posters had been produced at taxpayer expense by a professor who had cancelled her classes for a week just to organize the protest. Instead of attending the classes they paid for, students were given "extra-credit" for listening to their professors denigrate their president and their country.

I was pleased when some of the students who were offended took action by making hundreds of pro-war flyers that they posted all over campus. Unfortunately, university employees removed scores of them from the student union under the pretense that they were "offensive." Nonetheless, the same employees were not offended by dozens of magazines that were previously left in the same area by gay activists. Their literature was allowed to remain despite the fact that it contained a photograph of two gay men engaged in anal sex. Nor was there any effort to remove a large sign left by the Women's Resource Center earlier in the semester which called for all "P**sies" to unite and attend a feminist play called *The Vagina Monologues*.

Eventually, the promotion phase ended and the big day of the "walk out" finally came around. The main event, which was a panel of several faculty members discussing their opposition to the war, was attended by only a handful of peace activists. Most students who had their classes cancelled were probably taking in the sun at nearby Wrightsville Beach.

One conservative graduate student, as well as a conservative faculty member, decided to display mocking posters outside of the building where the faculty "discussion" panel was being held. One poster simply had pictures of women and children who had been murdered in chemical weapons attacks launched during Saddam's reign of terror. Another said, "Please go home American soldiers... Iraqis enjoy being raped, tortured, and gassed by Saddam."

Naturally, the "open minded" organizers of the event weren't too receptive to these dissenting opinions. In fact, one university employee (the male secretary of one of the organizing professors) called the police on the theory that the two silent protesters were not allowed to stand outside the building where the panel was being held.

When three police cars arrived, they got a lecture explaining the unconstitutionality of the provision in the university handbook delineating the outside of the building as a "no free speech zone." This only took about fifteen minutes with the help of a few US Supreme Court case citations and the promise of a lawsuit in the event of any arrests.

The day was all capped off with a rally under the university clock tower that featured an "open microphone" for students to express their views on the war. Despite the fact that pro-war students outnumbered the peaceniks, none were allowed to take the microphone to express their support of the war.

Fortunately, pro-war students organized their own rally two weeks later in response to the faculty-led peace protest. I was honored to be the only professor asked to speak at the event, even though openly pro-war professors are hard to come by at the university. Of course, before I spoke the university police had to remove sticks that were jammed into the electrical outlets by war protesters attempting to sabotage the rally. When I finally took the microphone, I noticed that the event was better attended than the anti-war rally. This, despite the fact that the university did not advertise the event on the university Web site like they had done for the peace rally.

During my speech, I shared a story I heard from an Iraqi woman who previously lived under Saddam's regime. She told of her neighbors having their tongues cut out for speaking out against the Iraqi dictator. She also told of the practice of forcing dissenters to watch while their children were raped and sodomized by Iraqi soldiers. In closing, I suggested that the best judges of the morality of the war in Iraq are the Iraqi citizens. Not socialist professors who decry American imperialism over four-dollar lattes.

Of course, my comments weren't well received by the local peace protesters. After sending me several e-mails calling me names too obscene to reprint, I felt rather relieved. After all, at least they didn't send viruses to crash my computer. That's what happened to a city councilman who dared to propose a resolution in support of the war.

Although the peace movement has suffered a few recent setbacks, they remain confident that they can construct a Utopian society. With their penchant for obscene messages, vandalism, and computer terrorism, they just might pull it off. If not, they can always become college professors.

UPDATE: The student who designed the anti-war poster found in my office was named as the most outstanding student leader at UNCW for the year 2002-2003. When I asked the student anti-war group (of which she is a member) to refrain from entering my office when I was not there, they asserted their absolute right to enter the office whenever they pleased. Their rationale: It isn't Dr. Adams' office. It belongs to the state.

Crash Landing for Affirmative Action?

Last month, I published an article that mocked affirmative action by suggesting a new grading system for my students at UNC-Wilmington. Under my satirical proposal, I suggested that white males should have points deducted and given to women and minorities in order to illustrate the injustice of current affirmative action policies in higher education.

After hearing me discuss it on the *O'Reilly Factor*, employees at Robins Air Force Base in Georgia contacted me, claiming that my proposal was actually a reality in at least one branch of the US Military. Subsequently, I received (from an anonymous employee) a copy of an e-mail ordering software division supervisor Harry Jennings to downgrade the performance evaluations of one white female and five white males. The e-mail also directed Jennings to add points to the performance appraisals of two minority males in order to "more balance the ethnic groups" in their annual evaluations. My first reaction to the e-mail was one of disbelief. Such blatant discrimination would be expected in the halls of academia but not within the ranks of the US military. However, upon subsequent investigation, I found that Jennings had admitted to the legitimacy of the e-mail to a reporter for the *Macon Telegraph* over a year ago. The incriminating e-mail seems to have been accidentally left on a shared computer drive at the Air Force base two years ago. Since then, it has managed to escape the attention of the national news media.

However, this evidence of racial discrimination in the name of affirmative action hasn't escaped the attention of six white male civilian employees at Robins, two of whom are Vietnam veterans. They have filed suit in federal court and are currently in the discovery phase for a trial expected to commence early next year. They plan to bring to court additional e-mails, which indicate that the performance appraisals of employees were actually reduced in compliance with the orders issued in the aforementioned e-mail.

They will also bring a lawyer with experience in at least one high profile affirmative action case. Lee Parks, an Atlanta attorney, won notoriety a few years ago when he successfully defeated the University of Georgia's admissions policy before a three-judge panel of the 11th Circuit Court of Appeals. The Board of Regents of the University of Georgia did not challenge Parks' decisive victory.

I spoke with Parks last week about his progress in the discovery phase of this important lawsuit. He stated that they have already uncovered evidence that the practice of tampering with performance evaluations in the name of "ethnic diversity" extends to Air Force bases throughout the entire Southern region of the United States. Other Air Force personnel have indicated that the practice may also extend to other regions, as well as other branches of the United States military.

Depending on the veracity of the plaintiff's claims, this is a case that could be as important as the one currently before the United States Supreme Court concerning admissions policies at the University of Michigan. However, it is important for a different reason. The Robins case raises no interesting legal issues. If the claims of the plaintiffs are correct, the legal judgment is easy. However, there are a number of extra-legal issues of greater importance.

First, and perhaps most important, is the issue of employee morale. It is difficult to imagine how the morale so necessary for national security can be maintained in a military that does not use merit as its sole basis for performance evaluations. Former Robins AFB supervisor George Allison told the *Macon Telegraph* that he knows morale has declined because, like others, he "... was not able to honestly evaluate (his) own employees" due to the minority quota system. Allison worked on the base for thirty years.

There is also a unique issue concerning the impact of this policy on Air Force personnel. Unlike those who are rejected from the University of Michigan School of Law, our military personnel cannot simply re-apply to another slightly less prestigious institution. They are usually induced into a long-term arrangement where they expect to be promoted on the basis of merit alone.

Furthermore, there is another matter of pure principle. Those who are not taught at home that it is wrong to lie and to falsify documents are taught these values by the United States Air Force. If military personnel are not upholding such values, there is more to be concerned about than sanctimonious hypocrisy. There are also legitimate national security concerns. People who lie about small matters (though this is no small matter) will lie about larger matters as well.

Many other issues will also be discussed if this case ever hits the mainstream national media. As of this writing, the story has escaped the radar screen of major news outlets like the *New York Times*. Before the recent controversy involving Jayson Blair, I wondered why.

The "False Friends" of the Court

The other day I was explaining the "false friends" doctrine to undergraduates in my criminal procedure class. Derived from the classic Supreme Court case of Hoffa v. United States (1966), the doctrine serves as a warning to citizens that the constitution does not always protect them when their friends turn out to be police informants.

The general principle of urging suspicion of those who present themselves as friends is advice that the Supreme Court should itself follow as it considers a record-breaking seventy-eight friend-of-the-court briefs in the University of Michigan (UM) affirmative action case. Evidence is beginning to suggest that some law schools are willing to lie in an effort to protect their admissions policies, all in the name of "diversity."

Recently, Indiana University (IU) School of Law submitted a brief to the Supreme Court in support of the UM admissions policy. The IU brief, signed by Admissions Committee Chair Jeffrey Stake, claims that the school "relies heavily" on LSAT scores and GPA for the "vast majority" of its admissions decisions. However, in an interview with the *Bloomington Herald Times*, Stake claims that only half of the admittees are selected primarily for having high LSAT scores.

In the same interview Stake adds, "It's not true that most of the lower LSAT scores belong to minority students." However, official school data indicate that white students at IU typically have an LSAT average surpassing the 80th percentile. The black average often falls below the 30th percentile. Stake also denies that IU has a minority quota system despite the fact that it has offered admission to 52, 52, and 53 black students over the last three years, respectively. Interestingly, the corresponding number of blacks applying to the law school over the last three years is 116, 161, and 207.

When asked to explain the very stable number of admissions offers to blacks despite a near doubling of black applicants in the last three years, Stake calls it a "coincidence." The IU amicus brief says that "(T)here is no goal to admit a certain number or percentage of people with particular characteristics."

Recently, former admissions committee member Robert Heidt took the courageous step of calling the school's bluff in an editorial to the *Indianapolis Star*. In the editorial, Heidt accuses the law school of imposing a de facto quota on the number of blacks and other minorities in each first-year class. In addition, he accuses the school of leapfrogging less qualified minority applicants over hundreds of candidates in a given year.

Much of the information that is now coming out about IU's questionable law school admissions policies is the result of public records requests made by Scott Dillon, a recent graduate of the program. These records have uncovered a number of interesting aspects of the selection process. For example, it is now clear that in the past IU has kept detailed records on the numbers of "minority applications received," "minority applicants presented to admissions committee," "number of admitted minority applicants," "number of denied minority applicants," "confirmed minority applicants," "minority applicants not coming," and "minority cancellations."

IU's brief to the Supreme Court claims that it doesn't presently keep track of how many minorities have outstanding offers or have accepted admission. That is fortunate since Jeffrey Stake has told the *Indianapolis Star* that he views quotas to be illegal, adding that he "would never consider achieving diversity by breaking the law."

As one might imagine, Dillon's efforts to reveal the truth about the law school's admissions policies have been poorly received. Recently, his efforts to disseminate information about the differential qualifications of white versus minority students were thwarted when over five hundred memos placed in student mailboxes were stolen within a day of their distribution. While the dean of the law school has acknowledged and condemned the theft, she refuses to remedy the situation by distributing the memo electronically to all members of the law school community.

Indiana is not the only law school that seems reluctant to reveal the truth about its admissions policies. I recently called the University of North Carolina at Chapel Hill (UNC) seeking an explanation for their decision to file a brief to the Supreme Court on behalf of UM. When I did, one of the school's administrators claimed that they did not use race at all in the admissions process. When asked how the UM case affected UNC's law school, her reply was simple: "Because we support diversity." When I later read their brief, I saw that the school described its policy as "race-conscious." In others words, they filed a brief because they really do consider race in admissions.

Although UNC's brief claims that the school uses race "carefully and sparingly," they contradict themselves repeatedly in subsequent portions of the brief. Specifically, they claim that a decision barring them from using race would result in a "return of de facto racial segregation" and a "re-emergence of regional apartheid." These are hardly consequences one would expect from abandoning a "careful" and "sparing" use of race.

Furthermore, UNC attempts to justify their continued use of "race-conscious" admissions by telling the Supreme Court that "doctors and hospitals offer lifesaving treatments differently, depending on the race of their patients." Though they offer no documentation supporting these claims, they do offer one simple remedy: race-based affirmative action at UNC School of Law.

I have no doubt that many of the briefs written to the Supreme Court in support of affirmative action are completely forthcoming and accurate. However, some are simply emotional appeals with little basis in reality. Others are deliberate distortions submitted in the name of social justice. But these briefs have one thing in common. They are all written by "friends of the court." At least that's how they present themselves.

So You're A Feminist?
... Isn't That Cute

Dear UNC-Wilmington Board of Trustees:

It has recently come to my attention that a feminist student at UNCW has taken offense to a sticker on my office door which reads, "So you're a feminist . . . Isn't that cute." I found this out after obtaining a copy of a letter her father wrote to the Board of Trustees. I could comment at some length on the obvious hypocrisy of her decision to ask her father to defend feminism for her, but I won't. Let me get straight to the point: I did not put that sticker on my office door.

This terrible misunderstanding is all the result of an experiment on diversity and tolerance that I decided to undertake several years ago. It all started when I noticed that a colleague of mine had a "Mondale/Ferraro '84" sticker on the filing cabinet in her office. I also noticed that another colleague had one posted on the front of his office desk.

Remembering that the university has a provision specifically prohibiting faculty from using "University funds, services, supplies, vehicles, or other property to support or oppose the candidacy of any person for elective public office . . .," I decided to initiate my experiment.

First, I placed a "Clinton/Gore '96" sticker prominently on my office door to see if anyone would take offense. After two years without any complaints, I decided to replace the sticker with one that said "George W. Bush for President." Within a few weeks I heard reports from two faculty members, as well as one staff member, saying that someone was preparing to file a complaint about the Bush sticker.

Since the faculty handbook specifies "appropriate disciplinary action, including discharge from employment" as one possible consequence of violating the aforementioned rule, I decided it was time to let the faculty in on my little experiment. I did this by sending an e-mail to everyone in the building, which began as follows: "You have all been involved in an experiment in tolerance which, unfortunately, some of you have failed . . ."

As you can imagine, the "liberal" Democrat who was conspiring to punish me for the Bush sticker decided to let the matter go. But, for me, the First Amendment fun was just beginning. After one animal rights activist heard about my little prank, she came by the office for a laugh. I put up an "I Love Animals, They're Delicious" sticker just for her. Some liberals really do have a sense of humor, you know.

Of course, others don't. After one of my feminist colleagues came by to say that she didn't mind my stickers as long as I didn't post anything "pro-life," I had to respond. That explains the picture on my door showing a newborn baby with "Is this the face of the enemy?" printed above his forehead. If you come by my office, you can't miss it. It's in bold letters.

There is one more thing I have to tell you before I reveal the source of the sticker that sparked this whole exchange. I have turned my door into a campus "free speech zone" by inviting all of my students to put their own bumper stickers on the door. That explains why most of the stickers aren't mine. It also explains why some seem to contradict others. For example, next to the "gay pride" sticker on my door, there is a giant pink one that reads, "Heterophobia is a social disease." I will admit to making that one, by the way.

But I had absolutely nothing to do with the *"Vagina Monologues"* sticker or the picture of Saddam Hussein below it. You may want to contact the Office of Diversity about those. Or maybe the Department of Middle Eastern Studies.

But back to the issue of the offended parent. If you would like, I can have the non-feminist student who placed the allegedly anti-feminist sticker on my door contact the feminist student who took offense. She would be glad to claim responsibility. Or perhaps her daddy can call the feminist's daddy and work everything out.

As for me, it's time to turn to some broader issues, such as fostering an appreciation for freedom of expression at our university. In fact, pretty soon you will be receiving my new proposal for First Amendment sensitivity training sessions for UNCW faculty and students. I might even amend the proposal to include parents as well.

As for encouraging the easily offended to approach college with a sense of humor, I haven't found a solution for that one. I guess all we can do is lead by example.

The Campus Crusade Against Christ (Revisited)

I would urge everyone reading this column, whether they are a Christian, a conservative, or simply a firm believer in our constitution to do two things without delay. First, read every word of this editorial carefully. Second, take the time to e-mail Chancellor James Moeser demanding appropriate personnel changes necessary to end the unconstitutional assault on religious organizations at the University of North Carolina at Chapel Hill.

I first wrote about the issue of anti-Christian bigotry on college campuses last July in an editorial entitled "The Campus Crusade Against Christ." The editorial attempted to draw attention to the hypocrisy of campus liberals who combat bigotry against certain groups while actually promoting bigotry against Christians. Despite using a somewhat humorous approach, my commentary was poorly received by many of my "open-minded" colleagues.

Early in January, I learned about an administrative threat to de-recognize InterVarsity Christian Fellowship (IVCF) at UNC-Chapel Hill. This threat, which would have effectively banned the student group from campus, was the result of their requirement that group officers subscribe to orthodox Christian principles. In other words, they would be allowed to remain on campus if they would only abandon their core beliefs and accept the official religion of UNC-Chapel Hill which is, of course, any religion which approves of homosexual conduct.

As a result of negative publicity generated by the indispensable Foundation for Individual Rights in Education (www.thefire.org), the threat against IVCF was rescinded in a letter written by Chancellor Moeser. In the letter, Moeser said that the conflict between the school's diversity policies and the First Amendment guarantee of freedom of religion was "not a simple matter."

Actually, it is a very simple matter. The First Amendment (found in the United States Constitution) trumps the "diversity policies" found in the handbooks of state-funded institutions of higher learning. Most of us learned this simple principle in our high school civics classes. Of course, university administrators often pretend that they don't understand basic principles that interfere with their efforts to promote "diversity" and "multiculturalism."

After the threat against IVCF was rescinded, I was informed by Wilmington attorney Charlton Allen that the *Daily Tar Heel* reported that over a dozen other threats of de-recognition had been issued to various student groups at UNC-CH. After filing a public records request, we obtained copies of the letters from Interim University Counsel Glenn George. Predictably, the threatening letters were overwhelmingly directed to Christian groups engaging in such transgressions as asking members to "model an appropriate Christian character" and hailing the importance of "discovering … what it means to have a relationship with Jesus Christ …" Allen and I summarized those letters in an editorial written in mid-January for *Breakpoint Online*.

Shortly thereafter, I made a public records request to UNC-CH asking for any similar letters that may have been written over the last ten years. As a result of substantial (and, in my view, unnecessary) delays in processing my request, I was forced seek help from Allen in getting the university to turn over the information. After a delay of over two months, we were successful.

Upon receipt of the requested documents, it became apparent that most of them were letters written after we made our request. Specifically, they were mostly requests for non-Christian student groups to amend their constitutions in order to comply with diversity requirements. For example, one group was asked to change its constitution to read "he/she" in places where it previously read "he" or "she." This may seem trivial to some. However, I interpreted it as an effort to mask a pattern of anti-Christian bias by creating hundreds of documents unrelated to interference with the expression of Christian values.

After sifting through 1,167 documents (mostly e-mails), we made a number of disturbing discoveries. They are summarized below:

- **In the fall of 1995,** The Muslim Student Association (MSA) was denied official recognition by the UNC Office of Student Activities for refusing to allow non-Muslims to hold office in the group. The university later reversed its decision in a letter to MSA that cautioned, "Assuming there will be no problems with your organization… recognition will extend until September 30, 1996."

The letter further cautioned the MSA, "it is critical that you inform the Office of Student Activities about changes within your organization" and that "failure to do so will result in loss of recognition."

- *On November 14, 1995*, Jonathan Curtis, assistant director of Student Activities, wrote the University Counsel asking whether an implied requirement that IVCF members must be Christians conflicts with university diversity requirements.

- *On November 29, 2002*, a member of the national Board of Directors of the Alpha Iota Omega Christian Fraternity complained to the university about its request that the fraternity amend its constitution to allow non-Christians to join. Internal memoranda indicate that the organization later capitulated.

- *On the same day*, Alpha Epsilon Omega Sorority notified the university that they were not willing to amend their constitution to permit homosexuals and members of different religions to join their Christian sorority. Three days later, Jonathan Curtis responded saying, "I will send a letter to the chapter by United States Postal Service informing you of the termination of (your) official recognition . . ."

- *On December 7, 2002*, the university announced that UNC law professor Glenn George would take over as Interim University Counsel in January of 2003.

- *On December 10, 2002*, Jonathan Curtis wrote 17 letters threatening UNC student groups with de-recognition. Thirteen letters were to religious groups. Twelve were Christian organizations.

- *On January 6, 2003*, Dean Bresciani, Interim Vice Chancellor for Student Affairs, wrote an e-mail to Jonathan Curtis asking for a copy of "the funding history for the 17 'bad boys'." In a "high importance" e-mail, Curtis wrote to Student Government Association (SGA) officers to formally advise them "regarding the possibility of freezing the funds of InterVarsity Christian Fellowship based on the recent issues raised about their governance." The issue was their insistence that IVCF officers subscribe to orthodox Christian principles.

- *On January 28, 2003*, Young Life was told to change their constitution to refer to its membership as a "community supporting Christianity" instead of "a community of adult Christians."
- *On the same day*, Jonathan Curtis wrote the Alpha Epsilon Pi Fraternity to thank them for amending their constitution so that they no longer described themselves as an organization that "believes in God."
- *On January 29, 2003*, the Lutheran Campus Ministry was told to change their constitution so that it no longer referred to its membership as a "Christian Community" but, instead, as a "Christ-centered community." Phi Beta Chi, a Lutheran sorority, was also given a similar mandate.

Sadly, the above list of unconstitutional demands is not exhaustive. Sadder still, the documents indicate that these demands were issued with both the knowledge and approval of the university's top administrators. It is hard to believe that UNC administrators are so profoundly ignorant of the Constitution that they do not recognize the illegality of their actions. It is more likely that they are simply political activists feigning ignorance of the Constitution in the name of "diversity."

Either way, the solution is clear. The nation's oldest public institution of higher learning needs new leadership.

Ridiculous Man–Hating Lesbians

Dear Women's Studies Professor:

I recently read the comments you made to a local newspaper during Women's History Month (WHM), which, I believe, used to be referred to as "March." It may surprise you to know that I agree with your assertion that the university used bad judgment in sponsoring a concert by the rapper Ludacris during WHM. I don't think there is ever a good time to have the rapper sing about "bi**es" and "hos" in the name of campus diversity.

I also agreed when you told the paper that it was unfortunate that many people view feminists as "ridiculous man-hating lesbians." Your suggestion that feminists should employ humor more often in order to combat that stereotype is certainly correct. Along those lines, I hope you don't mind me writing to make a few more suggestions that will help to erode that unfortunate stereotype.

First of all, I think that it was probably a mistake when you decided to hang posters around campus in protest of the Ludacris concert. I don't question your general right to hang posters but, instead, your specific choice in this instance. I am referring to one that you created which shows a woman kicking a man in the face in an apparent show of women's "empowerment." While mine is only one opinion, I think that others will agree that such a poster could actually promote the view of feminists as "ridiculous man-hating lesbians."

I was also disappointed that you paid for the posters with university funds. I also don't think it was wise to print "brought to you by the Women's Resource Center" on the bottom of the poster. The Center should combat *misogyny*, not promote *mrogyny*. Think about it.

For the time being, those are the only suggestions I have for you. However, I do hope you will pass on some advice to your colleagues who teach in Women's Studies. For example, I understand that one of your fellow professors nearly jeopardized her job five years ago when she prevented a male student from signing up for her Women's Studies class. Apparently, she thought it was safe to tell him that the class was only for women. When the male student in question told me this, I thought he was kidding. That was before another of your liberal colleagues, a self-described male feminist, confirmed his story.

Fortunately for the professor involved, the student was too intimidated to pursue a claim against her. But unfortunately, the professor's conduct reinforced the stereotype that feminists are, in your words, "ridiculous man-hating lesbians."

In addition to allowing them to sign up for your Women's Studies classes, it is important to be sensitive to the needs of the few men who actually do enroll. For example, I was told by the lone male student in a "Women and Literature" class that the professor stated (during her lecture) that after all her troubles with men, she now wished she had "converted" to lesbianism when she was younger. I didn't believe that one either until a woman taking the class confirmed it. And there were no remaining doubts after I read the professor's autobiography in which she spent countless pages attacking all of her former husbands. I hate to say it again, but this kind of behavior leads many to believe that feminists are merely "ridiculous man-hating lesbians."

I also want to point out that there are certain limitations on a professor's right to kick male students out of Women's Studies classes. I am in possession of a note written by the aforementioned "Women in Literature" professor to the lone male student in the class (there were thirty-six females enrolled). In the note, the professor asks the student to "reconsider (his) decision to take (the) class" for allegedly making comments that were "critical of the class subject matter."

Interestingly, the professor admits that she did not hear the comments but says nonetheless that they were "at odds with the purpose of the class," "completely unacceptable," and "damag(ing) the atmosphere (she was) working hard to create." Of course, he dropped the class for fear of failing. Now he thinks all feminists are "ridiculous man-hating lesbians."

But enough of the behavior of individual professors in your program. I also want you to reconsider some of the projects you undertake as a group. For example, I noticed that you petitioned against a campus appearance by the Dallas Cowboy Cheerleaders and that you later decided to sponsor a beauty pageant for obese women. Men's general preference for the former over the latter is probably here to stay. Better move on to another issue.

Finally, I was wondering if you could explain something: I heard one of your feminist colleagues take a pretty strong stand against breast implants for women the other day at lunch. I think she called them patriarchal and an unfamiliar term derived from phallus. After I reminded her that she was a gay activist who supports sex changes for men, I asked whether there was a contradiction. After all, men don't even have breasts to begin with. She told me "our contradictions make us human."

Maybe so. But her prejudices sure make her look ridiculous. But I agree that it doesn't mean she's a lesbian.

The Men's Resource Center

By now, readers of my editorials are sick and tired of my complaints about the antics of campus feminists. Many are undoubtedly wondering when I am going to stop criticizing and actually do something constructive. In response to my critics, I have decided to establish a new Men's Resource Center (MRC) at UNC-Wilmington.

As of this writing, I haven't actually gotten approval for the MRC, but I figure that the administration won't mind if I get things going without making any funding requests. Unlike the Women's Resource Center (WRC), I won't ask for an actual center. I'll just put a sign on my door (below the sticker that says "So you're a feminist... Isn't that cute") and get started right away using my own office. I will also pay for all invited speakers with the money I earn making fun of liberals in speeches I make on various college campuses. The taxpayers are really getting a bargain with my new MRC.

The principal purpose of my center will be to provide a safe haven or a comfort zone for men who feel that they are working and/or studying in a hostile environment. I first got the idea for these safe zones for men in the fall of 1994 while I was serving on the Sexual Assault Advisory Board. During one of our board meetings, a feminist student suggested mandatory rape awareness training for male students who were members of fraternities. Under her plan, fraternity members would face expulsion from the university if they refused to attend the classes.

I thought it would be nice to have a place where these men could go to get away from feminists who think that fraternity members are inclined to be rapists. In fact, six years later, a student of mine (a member of a fraternity) was falsely accused of raping a female student. After she retracted her accusation, the male student didn't have a special place where he could go to receive support from the trauma associated with his horrific ordeal.

Nor was there a safe haven for a philosophy professor at UNC-Wilmington who was viciously attacked by another professor in his department for his beliefs about the crime of rape. According to my conversations with both professors, their argument dealt with the issue of different degrees of rape. The feminist (and socialist) professor took the position that all rapes are equally bad. The man argued that there should be more than one degree of rape.

In order to support his position, he made a hypothetical comparison between the rape of a woman who was attacked in an alley and beaten severely versus a woman who consented to sex and then changed her mind at the last minute only to have the man proceed to penetrate. He simply concluded that the first scenario should be first-degree rape while the second scenario should constitute second-degree rape.

Despite the fact that the man's position was, and still is, the law in North Carolina and in most other states, the feminist professor decided to take the matter to the dean, seeking a reprimand and possible dismissal. It seems to me that he could have used a place to go and seek reassurance from someone who cares.

In the fall of 2000, another incident gave me insight into the possible benefit of having an MRC. The incident involved a student of mine who was trying to get out of her third consecutive test in my criminal justice class. There were only three tests altogether and I had already denied her twice. After I denied her the third time, she concocted a story about her sister being raped, beaten, and hospitalized in Winston-Salem, North Carolina. And, of course, no one in her family was available to visit her sister on her deathbed. Because I didn't believe her, she went to the Office of the Dean of Students, claiming that I was, among other things, insensitive to women.

Fortunately, an employee in the dean's office revealed her story as a hoax. She handled the incident like a true professional. However, the university didn't suspend or expel the student. I was told that another student had concocted a story of her own rape just to get out of taking a test. To the best of my knowledge, she wasn't expelled or suspended either.

After I finish this editorial, I'm going to hang that sign on my office door. Then I'm going to arrange my first two speakers for the fall semester. The first will be asked to give a lecture entitled, "The Politicalization of Rape by Feminist Professors." The second will give a lecture entitled, "When Women Cry 'Wolf,' Real Victims Suffer."

After that, I'll decide what to do next spring when the Women's Center sponsors *The Vagina Monologues* on "V-Day." Despite numerous requests, the MRC will not sponsor *The Penis Monologues*. At least, not on D-Day.

Narrow–Minded Religious Bigots

As I was browsing around my university's Web site last fall, I noticed an extensive list of recommended readings in a section labeled "spirituality" on the project B-Glad portion of the Web site. Project B-Glad is a taxpayer-funded educational project focusing on gay, lesbian, bisexual, and transgendered persons issues that is sponsored by the Office of Campus Diversity. Our chancellor signed the project into effect on September 11, 2001.

Perhaps I should commend our administration for remaining productive on a day when most Americans were mourning the loss of thousands in the terrorist attacks on the World Trade Center and the Pentagon. However, I am bothered by the fact that all of the religious readings that have been posted as part of the project have been pro-homosexual. (E.g., *Faith and Religion in the Lives of Gay Men*; *Lesbian, Gay, and Bisexual People within Organized Religion*; and about fourteen other books).

Because I wanted to see the university add some readings that reflect a different perspective, I wrote to our chancellor with a few suggestions. First, I advised him to insert a disclaimer at the top of the Project B-Glad "spirituality" section that says, "UNCW does not take a position on the question of whether homosexuality is compatible with the Bible."

After that, I asked him to add eight religiously based recommended readings that discuss the possible negative effects of homosexuality on various social institutions. (E.g., *Utopia Against the Family; Coming Out of Homosexuality;* and *Homosexuality and the Politics of Truth*).

Despite sending my requests by both regular mail and e-mail, I never heard back from the chancellor. As of this writing, the Office of Campus Diversity continues to post only pro-homosexual religious readings on its Web site. They also reinforce the idea of compatibility between homosexuality and religion with various highly paid campus speakers. For example, Mel White has been hired to assert compatibility between Christianity and homosexuality. Irshad Manji, a self-described "queer Muslim," has spoken on the compatibility between homosexuality and Islam. To my knowledge, no religious speaker has ever been paid to proffer a contrary view.

Additionally, since 1999 I have heard complaints from students who have applied to be student orientation leaders at UNCW. Specifically, several have reported that they were quizzed about their attitudes towards homosexuality during the application process. The students who spoke to me had religious objections to homosexuality that they kept to themselves during their interviews for fear of having their applications rejected. Of course, it is difficult to understand how attitudes towards homosexuality affect the ability to lead brief campus tours for prospective students during orientation.

More recently, it has come to my attention that diversity

proponents who specifically assert compatibility between Christianity and homosexuality have subjected students employed in various positions at my university to lectures. In a time of deep budgetary crisis, it is difficult to understand why the university pays for these lectures. Again, they promote only one view on this controversial and highly personal subject.

I hope that many who are reading this article have also read my recent article entitled "The Campus Crusade Against Christ (Revisited)," which documents the unconstitutional assault on religious student organizations at UNC-Chapel Hill. Readers of both articles may well conclude that an effort to establish homosexuality as the official state religion is well underway in the UNC system.

I also hope that readers will agree with my assertion that the UNC system is in need of a new form of sensitivity training. Towards that end, I will soon be proposing First Amendment sensitivity training sessions for university administrators on all sixteen UNC campuses. One of the main goals of the program will be to allow both individual students and campus religious groups to form their own opinions about the compatibility of homosexuality and religion. College administrators will be asked to tackle other issues like rising tuition costs.

I know that my initiative will be well received because UNC administrators care about the First Amendment. In fact, many said so last summer when they decried an attempt by the state legislature to block the use of "Approaching the Koran" in the summer reading program at UNC Chapel Hill. Many of those self-proclaimed defenders of academic freedom said that we must make sure that the UNC system is not controlled by narrow-minded religious bigots.

I certainly wouldn't want that to happen. But I'm afraid it already has.

Of Mice and Moeser

After several weeks of silence, Chancellor James Moeser has now responded to my recent charge that university administrators have been involved in an "unconstitutional assault on religious organizations at the University of North Carolina at Chapel Hill." His form response to my charge follows:

Thanks for sharing your views as a result of a recent Internet commentary about the university and an issue involving student organizations with religious affiliations that is some six months old and has been satisfactorily resolved. Permit me to provide some additional background information.

I think you will be pleased to learn that no religiously affiliated student organizations have lost their status as being officially recognized by the university. And, in fact, the university and the

Inter-Varsity Christian Fellowship reached a mutually satisfacto-
ry agreement in January after I reversed a previous action in
order to ensure that the IVCF would continue to operate as an
officially recognized student organization.

Thank you for the opportunity to provide additional context
regarding the issue.

Moeser's response seems to suggest that, 1) the issue was
fully resolved in January, 2) the issue was resolved amicably,
and 3) the issue was limited to chapters of IVCF. All three of
these assertions are demonstrably false.

My rebuttal to Chancellor Moeser will take the form of a
brief true/false examination. I expect that many readers of this
editorial will want to write the chancellor immediately,
demanding a direct answer to each of the following questions
(although readers will be provided with an answer key below):

1. ***True or False.*** UNC Chapel Hill's recent diversity com-
    pliance initiative began in December of 2002 by target-
    ing seventeen student organizations.
2. ***True or False.*** Thirteen of those organizations were reli-
    giously affiliated and twelve were Christian.
3. ***True or False.*** On December 2, Jonathan Curtis, assis-
    tant director of Student Activities, threatened the Alpha
    Epsilon Omega Christian organization with a letter of
    termination if they did not alter their constitution to
    conform to the university's diversity mission.
4. ***True or False.*** Curtis told the above organization to "slice
    and dice (their constitution) as the spirit moves you."
5. ***True or False.*** On January 28, 2003, Curtis thanked the
    president of the Alpha Epsilon Pi fraternity for modify-
    ing their constitution, so that it no longer described the

group as one that "believes in God."

6. ***True or False.*** In February, Young Life was told to remove the language "community of adult Christians" from their constitution.

7. ***True or False.*** In February, a UNC-CH professor complained to Curtis, concerning the "unconstitutional" harassment of yet another UNC-CH Christian organization (Carolina Hope).

8. ***True or False.*** In a February letter to University Counsel Glenn George, the above professor accused the university of engaging in "petty, demeaning, and bullying" behavior towards student organizations.

9. ***True or False.*** In February, a member of the Phi Beta Chi Christian sorority communicated their refusal to allow women of all religions to join their sorority, which they described as a "social sorority with Christian ideals." Jonathan Curtis informed them that he "very much regret(ed) hearing their decision." He then passed the matter on to the Office of University Counsel.

10. ***True or False.*** The President of Chi Alpha Omega Christian Fraternity wrote Chancellor Moeser in February to inform him that they had been threatened with de-recognition. This was after the "reversal" of the threat against IVCF.

11. ***True or False.*** The above-stated letter to Moeser complained that Chi Alpha Omega had not been given the same reprieve as Inter-Varsity.

12. ***True or False.*** On February 11, Chi Alpha Omega threatened James Moeser with a lawsuit for interfering with their "first amendment (sic) rights to freedom of religious exercise and freedom to peaceably assemble."

13. ***True or False.*** On February 10, the president of Phi Beta Chi wrote to Jonathan Curtis, pleading for advice on

how their Christian sorority could satisfy UNC's non-discrimination policy without "giving up what we stand for as a Christian group of women."

Answer Key: 1) True 2) True 3) True 4) True 5) True 6) True 7) True 8) True 9) True 10) True 11) True 12) True 13) True.

I hope that readers won't mind if I add the following multiple-choice question to the exam: Chancellor James Moeser, a) does not understand that the First Amendment trumps the diversity policies of UNC-CH, b) does not know that student religious groups were harassed at UNC-CH after his January "reversal" of the threats issued against IVCF, c) does not mind lying to the public in order to promote "diversity" at UNC-CH, d) all of the above, or e) none of the above.

I **won't** provide a key for that one. We already know the answer.

How I Lost My Virginity

First of all, you should be ashamed of yourself for reading this editorial. This is not an appropriate topic for a conservative commentary. Of course, it is an appropriate topic for a Women's Studies lecture. Let me explain.

I was sitting in Barnes and Noble one afternoon reading a book I didn't want to buy. The book cost seven dollars and I was on my tenth two-dollar coffee. I think it was by Tolstoy. At any rate, these two college students were talking about their "Women in Literature" class (over four-dollar lattes) when one turned to the other and said the following: "I just finished the assigned book for our class. I thought it was just so poignant. I agreed with our professor when she talked about the humiliation you feel after a man finishes ejaculating."

After reading the same line in *War and Peace* four times, I decided it was time to really concentrate. Not on Tolstoy, but on eavesdropping. I then realized that the two students were talking about a book, entitled *Intimate Reading: A Contemporary Women's Memoir*, by one of UNCW's self-described feminist scholars.

That day in Barnes and Noble, I considered buying the memoir. However, I didn't get around to doing so until recently when the author declined my invitation to join a panel I was organizing on the topic of abortion. She told me that she didn't want to discuss such a personal matter in public. That's when I decided to buy her book.

When I first opened the book, I noticed that in the acknowledgments she thanked her children as well as her husband for taking the time to read her memoir. The fact that they had read it wasn't significant until I read the first chapter, which detailed her first sexual encounter at age sixteen with her then-boyfriend, Alec.

After writing about the sexual encounter in fairly graphic terms, including her efforts to scrub her blood off of the stained couch, the author added that she had an important realization as she was bathing afterwards; "Only then, as I watched the thin thread of blood still weaving out of my vagina, dissipating into the scalding water, did it occur to me that he might have ejaculated inside of me."

She then told of dumping Alec after their lone sexual encounter, which took place after a year of going steady. She said that she was relieved to be "freed from his sexual persistence" and thus, capable of finding "uncomplicated fun." But things didn't work out that way.

Like so many others who begin to assess the consequences of unprotected sex after the encounter, the sixteen-year-old future scholar became pregnant. The book then launched into an attack on her parents for refusing to break the law (this was before Roe v. Wade) and take her to another country (like

Mexico) for a "humane abortion." Of course, the phrase "humane abortion" is an oxymoron. Sort of like "jumbo shrimp" or "feminist scholar."

Nonetheless, she then writes about having the baby and giving it up for adoption. The rest of the book is largely an account of how her parents' decision to force their conservative principles (i.e., their pro-life position) on her has ruined her life.

In the process of building her central thesis, she criticizes her first husband harshly, although she admits leaving him for her boss—the manager at a restaurant where she worked—after they had known each other for less than two weeks. By the way, she decided to marry the boss, but that didn't work out either. Of course, she let him have it in the memoir, too. But she did take it fairly easy on husbands three and four. And she actually praised her fifth husband. (I think this is all correct but I started to lose count. Seriously.)

I think she likes the last husband because he was nice enough to forgive a "highly sexualized friendship with another man" prior to their marriage. According to her, the "sexualized friendship" was caused by her dishonesty. Of course, her dishonesty was caused by her shame, which was caused by her parents making her have that baby at sixteen instead of getting an abortion. But, later, when the nice husband falsely accuses her of an affair, they both decide that his suspicion was due to "his own psychological shortcoming."

Although I would not recommend *Intimate Reading* to anyone suffering from depression, the memoir does end on a positive note when the author finally meets the daughter she was prevented from illegally aborting by her conservative parents. She also meets the grandchild her daughter had given her.

Indeed, there are numerous conservative lessons in this feminist memoir that seem completely lost upon its author. That one can reap priceless rewards by choosing adoption over abortion; that one must take responsibility for one's conduct at all times; and that one should avoid sexual intercourse until one understands its consequences are among those rewards.

Of course, today's university is one of the last places where you can expect to find a serious discussion involving critical self-examination. All too often, students are encouraged to sit around and talk about their feelings. Getting them in touch with their inner child is seen as the best way to achieve the paramount goal of giving them a positive self-image.

So remember, if you would rather talk about your feelings than read a great work of literature, go get yourself a four-dollar latte at Barnes and Noble. Or get a four-year degree in Women's Studies.

Author's Note: The author of *Intimate Reading* was awarded a prestigious Distinguished Teaching Award at UNCW. Several years later, she was given the award again. Thus, she is a Distinguished Distinguished Professor of English.

Uncle Tom's Cuban

I used to consider white liberals who praise Fidel Castro to be the most despicable people imaginable. That's probably because I have to deal with these people on a regular basis. I call them Starbuck's Socialists. You know the type. They spend about ten dollars a day to have other people make their coffee while they read the $20 deluxe edition of *The Communist Manifesto* at Barnes and Noble. They also spend a fortune to send their children to private schools with other white kids. Most of them are college professors.

But now I've changed my mind. I've decided that black liberals who praise Fidel Castro are just as repugnant. This change of heart follows my recent discovery that NAACP President Kweisi Mfume has struck trade agreements with the Cuban dictator after a "good will and trade mission" to the communist nation. In fact, this happened in November of

2002, but I don't remember reading about it. That was back when I was reading the *New York Times*.

However, in a November 12 NAACP press release, Mfume explained that his purpose in visiting Cuba was to "lend support to black farmers in the United States who would like to win export contracts with (Cuba)" and "to build a bridge between the NAACP and the people of Cuba, many of whom are descendants of Africa." Mfume also announced a meeting with the Central Committee of the Communist Party of Cuba.

In a November 14 NAACP press release, Mfume explained why he wanted to meet with communist leaders in Cuba: "(W)e hope to learn more about Cuba's education and health care systems, which offer free schooling and medical care to all citizens." The press release added "Although the US has some of the best health care facilities and physicians in the world, African Americans continue to have a shorter average life span than whites..."

To his credit, Mfume did meet with Cuban dissidents (although it took some persuading by the mayor of Miami). After the meeting, the NAACP reported that "(T)he dissidents claim that under the leadership of... Castro, the Cuban people are denied freedom of expression and freedom of religion." Furthermore, the NAACP reported, "The dissent leaders said they had been imprisoned and harassed by the government at one time or another because of their efforts to organize and call for change within Cuba." This quote was inserted only after noting that (the dissident leaders) "freely expressed their views to the NAACP delegation." The press release also ended with a quote from the National Assembly of the People's Power: "Most of these people (dissidents) just pretend to represent organizations. They have absolutely no support in our country."

There are two reasons why I find Mfume's Cuban visit to be disturbing. First, it was unnecessary. Intelligent people can realistically assess the likely impact of communism on the plight of African Americans by examining the effects of socialist policies that have been adopted in the United States.

For example, it is no coincidence that the Great Society initiatives of President Johnson were followed by skyrocketing rates of illegitimacy among African Americans. That rate is now at 70 percent. Interestingly, a search for the word "illegitimacy" yields no results on the NAACP Web site.

Nor does www.naacp.org have anything to say about the disproportionate number of black babies aborted in the United States. After thirty years of modeling our reproductive policies after the communists, we are approaching a total of fifty million abortions in post-Roe America. When we do pass that mark, about 20 million of the abortions will have been performed on black babies. If abortions were performed equally across racial groups that number would be around six million.

A second basis of objection to Mfume's visit to Cuba is its blatant hypocrisy. His willingness to pretend that human rights violations do not exist in order to advance economic interests—moreover agricultural interests—shows that he has indeed learned a lot from the institution of slavery. Namely, that freedom is expendable when it conflicts with the economic interests of the rich and powerful. Mfume is both.

Black America can do without communism and socialism just as it can do without affirmative action and reparations for slavery. And it certainly has no need for dictators like Fidel Castro and Kweisi Mfume.

The Viagra Monologues

I have been meaning to read *The Vagina Monologues* (TVM) ever since my university began sponsoring the feminist play several years ago in an effort to promote respect for women. Last week I finally found the time to read it in its entirety. I'll never be the same.

In the very first chapter of TVM, author Eve Ensler tells the reader that she wrote the controversial play because she "was worried about what we think about vaginas..." and because she "was worried about (her) own vagina. It needed a context of other vaginas—a community, a culture of vaginas." I suppose it takes a village to raise a vagina.

Ensler got the information for her play by talking to other women about their vaginas. One of the questions she asked over two hundred women was "if your vagina got dressed, what would it wear?" Responses from the women who agreed to be interviewed included, "A beret," "A leather jacket," "Lace and combat boots," and "An electrical shock device to keep unwanted strangers away." Nothing shocking there.

In addition to the questions she posed to all interviewees, Ensler did some focused interviews. One was with a woman who participated in a "vagina workshop." This is not to be confused with the "C*** Workshop" offered at Wesleyan University (their motto begins: "At Wesleyan, we aim high"). In this revealing chapter, the vagina student describes the director of the workshop as one who "helps women see their own vaginas by seeing other women's vaginas."

In fact, she helped her change her view of her own vagina. She had previously seen it as "an anatomical vacuum randomly sucking up particles and objects from the surrounding environment" and an "independent entity, spinning like a star in its own galaxy." Vacuum? Vagina? Vortex? It's all so confusing.

Later, after being unable to locate her clitoris with a handheld mirror, the vagina student was reassured by the director that her "clitoris was not something (she) could lose." I thought that was pretty insensitive to transgendered persons.

Another chapter urges women to spend time looking at their vaginas in order to love them. Here, the reader learns that vagina hatred is a part of the internalized hatred of the patriarchal culture. The book explains, "Like, if we'd grown up in a culture where we were taught that fat thighs were beautiful, we'd all be pounding down milkshakes and cookies." Or, like, maybe, they'd just, like, watch the Anna Nicole Show. Or, like, maybe something else.

Nonetheless, Ensler calls for vaginal unity by urging all "p******" to "unite." And some have listened to her by forming "c*** clubs" on college campuses. Some of you may have heard them on your campus chanting "viva la vulva!"

"My Angry Vagina" is perhaps the most disconnected chapter of TVM. The first few pages offer a diatribe against tampons. It then moves into a discussion of the prospect of talking vaginas capable of doing "vagina impressions." Imagine changing your impression of Groucho Marx to Monica Lewinsky with no additional props. The possibilities are endless!

A chapter called "The Little Coochie Snorcher That Could" chronicles the seduction of a sixteen-year-old girl by a twenty-four year old woman. Another chapter explores women's answers to the following question: "What does your vagina smell like?" Answers range from "wet garbage" to "God." Next thing you know, we'll have a play called "Irma La Douche."

Perhaps the highlight (or lowlight) of TVM is an interview with a six-year-old girl, which asks (among others) the following questions: "If your vagina got dressed, what would it wear?" "If it could speak, what would it say?" and "What does your vagina smell like?" Of course I wondered why Ensler would ask these questions of a six-year-old girl. Maybe she got the idea from Michael Jackson. Well, maybe not.

After nearly 120 pages of this obscenity, the author does ponder the possible ill effects of her research by asking whether "talking about vaginas ruin(s) the mystery." But then she dismisses that conclusion as "another myth that keeps vaginas in the dark, keeps them unknowing and unsatisfied." Finally she admits, "I realize I don't know what's appropriate. I don't even know what that word means. Who decides?"

Of course, many people would like to see TVM banned from college campuses. I disagree with that approach. Instead, I'm going to write my own play called *The Viagra Monologues*. That way, I won't be accused of censoring campus feminists. And I won't have to interview six-year-old boys.

Our New Class Policies

Dear Students:

Welcome back! It has been a long summer, and we are eager to start another year at the university. Before we begin, take the time to read this memo carefully as there have been some significant changes in our class policies since last semester.

As each student already knows, our university has expanded its commitment to diversity in recent years. This movement towards diversity has been inspired by the idea that a quality education is best achieved by bringing together heterogeneous groups who share different perspectives on a broad range of issues.

The diversity movement has increasingly called into question the idea of absolute truth and, to a lesser extent, objective reality. The core concept of diversity was given heightened legitimacy with this summer's landmark Supreme Court decision upholding the use of race-based affirmative action in higher education. (See Grutter v. Bollinger, 2003.) These new class policies were crafted in order to better promote the "compelling interest in diversity" that was the focal point of the *Grutter* decision.

In order to implement these changes, it will be necessary for each student to respond to the following questions concerning race, gender, and sexual orientation:

1. Which of the following best describes your race or ethnicity: a) white, b) black or African-American, c) Hispanic, d) Asian, e) multi-racial, or f) other?
2. Which of the following best describes your gender: a) male, b) female, c) undecided, or d) other?
3. Which of the following best describes your sexual orientation: a) heterosexual, b) homosexual, c) bisexual, d) heterosexual transgendered, e) homosexual transgendered, f) questioning, or g) other?

After each student has answered the above questions, the information will be transferred to an index card that will be used to identify the student's perspective during class discussion. In fairness, your instructor will keep a card reading "white heterosexual male" on his desk at all times. Students will receive credit for classroom participation only when these cards are displayed on the student's desk. This will ensure that other students are able to identify the perspective of each participant in classroom discussion.

Students will be asked to phrase class comments in a manner that reflects the perspective of their group without reference to antiquated notions of individual belief or opinion. For example, "we think" and "we believe" are appropriate introductions to classroom remarks, while phrases such as "I think" and "I believe" are unacceptable. Please remember that we are not interested in you as an individual. Group identity is our sole point of reference.

Because of our movement away from the idea of absolute truth, there will be some changes in class grading policies. Specifically, each group's performance on individual test questions will be analyzed after individual scores are computed. When it has been determined that a majority of a particular group has selected one of the "wrong" answers, the entire group will be given credit for the question. In other words, if the other answer is true for the group, its members will not be bound by the reality of the group responsible for producing the test. Note that in this particular course, white heterosexual males will not have the option of appealing, since they already have the advantage of taking a test that is written from their perspective.

Also note that students who are the sole representative of a particular group will automatically receive a score of 100 percent on every test, since such a student always constitutes a majority of the group that he/she/undecided/other represents. While this seems "unfair" at first glance, it is justified by the unique contribution such a student brings to the classroom.

The rules concerning "cheating" will also be relaxed starting this semester. The idea of "cheating" places too high a premium on the notion of truth. Furthermore, it is absurd to claim that a person "stole" an answer from someone else. Ideas belong to groups, not people. Therefore, during examinations each student will be allowed to consult with other members of the group to which he/she/undecided/other belongs.

Finally, there will be no rules concerning the antiquated concept of "plagiarism." While the courts still cling to the notion that ideas are the "property" of individuals, the university has a more sophisticated view. Nonetheless, we are confident that the courts will eventually change their opinion on this matter. Although they are often slow, the courts always follow the trends of academic elites when re-interpreting well-established legal doctrines.

Undoubtedly, many students will have apprehensions concerning these changes. But rest assured that we have less to fear now than we did when we were individuals.

My New Affirmative Action Hiring Proposal

Dear Lee:

I have been meaning to write you ever since you first expressed your disappointment with the lack of diversity among the faculty at UNC-Wilmington. I'm sure you remember our conversation three years ago when you decided to change your major from political science, because they didn't have a single Republican professor. You also told me that you raised the issue with one of your Democratic professors. I am sorry that he sarcastically responded to your complaint by saying that the department had a "careful screening process" which ensured that no Republican would ever be offered a tenure-track position. If that quote is accurate, it is a real sign of immaturity, not to mention intellectual insecurity. I think it was wise to seek another major.

I'm only sorry that I was unable to help you find an alternate major offering you a more diverse education as you prepared for law school. I thought that English would be a suitable alternative, but my research revealed that none of their thirty-one full-time professors were registered Republicans. I also looked into philosophy and religion, anthropology, and sociology and found that there were no Republicans in any of those departments. Finally, I considered complaining to the chancellor, but he was attending a Democratic fund-raiser the day I tried to reach him. My research also revealed that none of his seven vice-chancellors were Republicans.

For a long time afterwards, I must confess that I had given up on the prospect of creating a more diverse intellectual climate at our university. But, recently, my friend Jon Sanders at the John Locke Foundation in Raleigh wrote an article that explains how the *Grutter* decision may actually help conservatives remedy the lack of ideological diversity on college campuses.

After reading Sanders' article, I re-read *Grutter* and came to the same conclusion. After all, the Supreme Court did say that universities have a compelling interest in diversity. They also said that preferences aimed at fostering diversity were justified by historical discrimination. If such a rationale can be used to justify preferential treatment for minorities applying for admission as students, it would seem to apply to conservatives applying for teaching positions. Affirmative action for conservative professors would clearly help to create a more diverse intellectual climate. It would also go a long way towards remedying years of oppression experienced by conservatives at the hands of intolerant university leftists.

In order to test this new application of *Grutter*, I have created a questionnaire that I hope will be used to bring more conservative professors into higher education. I promise that this test will not be used as a device to "discriminate." Unlike student admissions policies, I will recommend its use only as a tiebreaker when universities are deadlocked on a hiring decision. I have noticed that there are a lot of these ties between equally qualified applicants. Usually the tie is between a white male and either a woman or a racial minority.

From now on, black women will not be the automatic winners in these situations. Under my plan, getting the job will depend on the applicant's performance on a test that directly measures attitudes. No longer will hiring decisions be based on assumptions about the manner in which attitudes correlate with certain demographic characteristics. My proposed test follows in its entirety:

Pick the best answer among the following options:
1. My last meal: a) had at least one type of food that had parents, or b) was comprised solely of vegetables.

2. The most evil leader of the 20th Century was: a) Joseph Stalin or, b) Ronald Reagan.

3. If a burglar broke into my house this evening I would rather: a) shoot him, or b) find out why he hated me.

4. It is morally reprehensible to: a) abort an eight-month-old human fetus, or b) slaughter a chicken for human consumption.

5. I am firmly convinced of the existence of: a) moral absolutes, or b) global warming.

6. I am more likely to watch: a) Fox News, or b) Al Jazeera.

7. If I were sitting on a runway for several hours inside an American Airlines jet that was experiencing "temporary technical problems," I would want a copy of: a) *Treason*, by Ann Coulter, or b) *Living History*, by Hillary Clinton.

8. The best way to invest for retirement is with: a) an IRA,

or b) social security.

9. The Constitution guarantees each adult the right to: a) bear arms, or b) engage in homosexual sodomy.

10. Kindergartners should never hear this word in the classroom: a) vagina, or b) God.

After completing the test, the number of times each applicant circled "a" will be computed. A higher number of "a" responses represents a greater contribution to faculty diversity (i.e., a more conservative applicant). If both applicants get the same score on the test, the hiring decision will be determined by a simple coin toss.

Remember Lee, I am proposing this test to benefit people like you who believe that their parents wasted tens of thousands of dollars on an education that promised diversity and delivered indoctrination. But also remember that I am only proposing this test as a tiebreaker. I promise that it will never become a part of all hiring decisions. Furthermore, I expect that 25 years from now, the use of such a test will no longer be necessary.

PART THREE

Intellectual Terrorism in the Wake of 9/11

In Dedication to an Undivided Humanity

September 11, 2001:

Few people will ever be able to forget where they were or what they were doing on the day that New York City and Washington, D.C. were attacked by the al-Qaida terrorist network. I was sitting in my office preparing for a 9:30 lecture in my Criminal Law and Procedure class. My girlfriend called after the first plane hit the World Trade Center. Seconds later, she exclaimed, "Oh my God, another one just hit the other tower. What's going on here?" I knew the answer before she finished her sentence.

When I walked into class just minutes later, I asked the students to give me their full attention. I began my lecture by saying, "I will do everything in my ability to finish this class period but it seems that, at the very least, we will have to leave early today. Airplanes have struck both of the towers of the

World Trade Center. There are reports of bombs going off in other parts of New York City. It is also rumored that the State Department has been attacked. In all probability, World War III is underway." Thankfully, some of those rumors were false. Nonetheless, I had the students' attention.

My two o'clock class was canceled, as was my six o'clock night class. On Thursday, I made no effort to talk about anything other than the situation in the Middle East. I told my students that we would try to pick up where we left off in the following week.

September 17, 2001:

It was a long weekend, without much rest. When I checked my e-mail for the first time in several days, I noticed that the messages had piled up. I looked up and down the address list trying to decide which one to open first. One message was from a student named Rosa Fuller. She was the daughter of Philosophy Professor Patti Turrisi, who also directs the Center for Teaching Excellence at UNCW. The subject line next to her address read "In Dedication to an Undivided Humanity."

I had taught Rosa the year before in an introductory course in criminal justice. She had never e-mailed me before. In fact, she didn't say much in class. She usually just sat back, dressed in black, wearing a beret and leather boots with her arms crossed. She seemed to take offense on one occasion to a remark I made about a communist named Benjamin Gitlow. We were covering his famous Supreme Court case, Gitlow v. New York (1925), and I believe I called him a "liberal pinko commie," but I meant no offense. After all, he had been dead for quite some time. I must have assumed there were no communists in the audience. I would later learn that I was wrong.

When I opened Rosa's message, I read the following:

To the students and faculty of the University of North
Carolina at Wilmington:

*The summary murder of thousands of people on the
morning of September 11th was a tragedy for the entire
human species. It was an irrational act that can only serve
the cause of irrationality. As we are members of a university, all irrationality deserves from us unequivocal condem-
nation. This is the place where, above all else, rationality
must be kept alive. We must keep discussion alive. We must
untiringly examine causes and effects, and not allow feelings of anger or depression to permanently cloud our vision.
In light of this, we must not for a moment forget the following: (1) the US government has been engaged in a combination of occupation and imperialist warfare in the
Middle East, aimed at domination of its oil resources, for
nearly two decades; (2) the US government gives its
unequivocal support to Israel's assassination of Palestinians
who are 'suspected' of being terrorists, falsely claiming that
any opposition to murder committed in the name of the
Israeli government amounts to Nazism; (3) as the World
Socialist Web site put it "far from America being 'the
brightest beacon for freedom and opportunity in the world,'
the US is seen by tens of millions as the main enemy of their
human and democratic rights, and the main source of their
oppression. The American ruling elite, in its insolence and
cynicism, acts as if it can carry out its violent enterprises
around the world without creating the conditions for violent
acts of retribution" and; (4) "both bin (sic) Laden and the
Taliban Muslims, whom the US accuses of harboring him,
were financed and armed by the Reagan-Bush administration to fight pro-Soviet regimes in Afghanistan in the
1980s. If they are involved in Tuesday's operations, then the*

American CIA and the political establishment are guilty of having nurtured the very forces that carried out the bloodiest attack on American civilians in US history"; (5) innocent Arab and Muslim Americans, including children, are being attacked and threatened in the chauvinist, racist fervor stirred by the war-mongering US media; (6) whatever their true feelings, the Bush administration stands, in several respects, to benefit from the results of the 'attack on America': (i) the current situation serves as a distraction from the fact that President Bush was illegally appointed to office by the reactionary majority of the US Supreme Court, through suppression of votes, in stark violation of the US constitution (sic), and (ii) the current crisis serves as justification, to the American people, for the continuation and intensification of US imperialist repression already in progress throughout the world.

The future is not about revenge, but about life. A humanity worth fighting for is a humanity undivided by petty nationalistic, imperialist, bourgeois squabbling. When this squabbling takes the form of all out war and the deaths of untold thousands of 'Americans' and 'foreigners,' the struggle for rationality is transformed into the struggle between life and death. The time for silence has ended; the time for rational discussion is now.

If you support open, unbiased, democratic discussion of all the facts, please forward this e-mail to friends and acquaintances both on and off campus. For more detailed information, see www.wsws.org.

> *Thank you for your time,*
> *Rosa Fuller.*

I don't have to tell you what I was thinking after I read Rosa's "rational" account of the events of September 11th.

Thousands of American bodies were still burning and two of my friends from New York City were missing when I received Rosa's "dedication." Nonetheless, I resisted the temptation to fire off an immediate response. I walked around the department, fuming, while another professor who knew Rosa told me that I shouldn't let it anger me, since that was the obvious intent of the missive. So I just forwarded the message to some friends like Rosa asked. Of the six people to whom I forwarded the response, several responded to me with outrage over the content of the message. I then wrote Rosa the following response, not knowing that it would eventually be quoted on national talk radio and on national television:

> *I will certainly forward this to others, and I hope they will respond. My response will be brief as your "statement" is undeserving of serious consideration. Your claimed interest in promoting rational discussion is dishonest. It is an intentionally divisive diatribe. The Constitution protects your speech just as it has protected bigoted, unintelligent, and immature speech for many years. But, remember, when you exercise your rights, you open yourself up to criticism that is protected by the same principles. I sincerely hope that your bad speech serves as a catalyst for better speech by others.*

I felt better after writing that and didn't give the matter much thought for the next couple of days. It certainly never occurred to me that my response could be interpreted by anyone as falling outside the protection of the First Amendment.

September 20, 2001:
A university employee called my office to tell me that Dr. Turrisi was overheard in Hoggard Hall telling a staff member

that she and her daughter were initiating an investigation of me for "verbally abusing" Rosa and for forwarding her e-mail to other people who supposedly did the same. According to the employee, Turrisi had stated that I had "no right" to forward Rosa's e-mail to other people. (Take a moment to re-read the end of Rosa's e-mail.) Turrisi had also apparently said that Rosa had sent the message only to me. Of course, she knew that wasn't true because it was sent to seventeen addresses, including Dr. Patti Turrisi's. It was also addressed "To the students and faculty of the University of North Carolina at Wilmington."

The Sociology and Criminal Justice secretary later informed me that Dr. Turrisi had called the department, angrily demanding to talk to my chair, Cecil Willis. When I went into Cecil's office, he said that Turrisi had called him directly and demanded to know who I sent the e-mail to and whether I had tried to "influence the discussion" of Rosa's e-mail. I told Cecil that it was not a crime (in fact, it's my job) to "influence discussion." I also told him to tell Turrisi that my e-mail communications were none of her business.

When I got back to my office, I called Thor Halvorssen at the Foundation for Individual Rights in Education (FIRE), a Philadelphia civil liberties organization that specializes in free speech and due process issues in higher education. I told him that a member of the administration was trying to launch an investigation against me for exercising my First Amendment rights. After I filled him in on the rest of the facts, he told me to call back if I heard from anyone in the administration besides Turrisi. That call came the next day.

September 21, 2001:
Sometime during the middle of the afternoon, I received a call from Provost John Cavanaugh. He immediately informed

me that Rosa Turrisi Fuller had filed a complaint against me. He then read the following complaint over the phone:

> *A University faculty member, Mike Adams, sent me an e-mail message, dated September 17, 2001, with the use of the University's central computing facilities and services, from the address adamsm@uncwil.edu, which berated me, with no semblance of an argument, with abusive epithets, which falsely represented me as "dishonest," "intentionally divisive," "bigoted," "unintelligent," and "immature." The intent of such a message is intimidation and defamation. I have reason to believe Adams may have sent copies of his false representation of me to others, inside and outside the University community, with the use of the University's central computing facilities and services. I, therefore, ask the Office of Information Technology, and any other appropriate office or officer, to let me and my representatives inspect the e-mail message Adams sent, from September 15 to September 18, as public business, in accordance with the Public Records Law of the State of North Carolina. If it is found that Adams sent his false representation of me to others, inside or outside the University community, and if these others acted on his false representation, and sent me abusive e-mail messages, then I shall also accuse him of libel.*

What I had just heard from the provost was all so absurd that I assumed he had called just to let me know about the complaint and to assure me that it would be dismissed immediately. But that isn't what happened. Instead he said that it wasn't a "good idea" to make students look bad. After assuring me that the administration had not yet gone into anyone's e-mail account, he asked if there was "anything (he) needed to know" about the contents of my e-mail folder before he and the administration defended me against her complaint. I told the provost that I didn't understand the question.

After asserting my absolute objection to anyone ever reading my private e-mail correspondence, I told the Provost that Turrisi was on a witch hunt that was motivated by her distaste for conservatives. I ridiculed the idea that I was somehow responsible for an apparent flood of negative responses to her daughter's e-mail. I suggested that if anyone had threatened Rosa, she should call the campus police. I also mocked him by stating that it would be a "good idea" to tell Turrisi to call off her investigation as I was prepared to bring out the big guns if she continued. By that I meant the FIRE and the national press, if necessary.

Later that afternoon I called Thor Halvorssen again. He urged me to e-mail the Provost to clarify my position and get a summary of our conversation on record. I took his advice. He also told me to start keeping a record of everything relating to the controversy. You are reading that record now.

September 24, 2001:

At about eight in the morning, I got a call from my girlfriend, Krysten Scott (now Krysten Adams), telling me that she had been called in to talk to the UNCW police about an allegedly "threatening message" she had sent to Rosa Fuller. Krysten is a 5'3", 115 lb., blue-eyed blonde alumnus of UNCW. She was working at the UNCW computing center and was taking classes at UNCW in order to obtain a teaching certification as she was in the process of a career change. Her mother had been awakened by a call from the police that she then relayed to Krysten.

When she went down to the police station, they assured her that there was no problem. The message she sent Rosa, which

said, in part, "People like you...deserve to be dragged down
the street by your hair" was not really an imminent threat.
Aside from containing other speech that was clearly political
in nature, there was no evidence that the message conveyed a
real intention to actually drag Rosa down the street. That's
hard to do at 115 lbs. Although she failed to win the sympa-
thy of the police, Rosa was far from finished.

September 26, 2001:
Harold M. (Hal) White, Jr., the university counsel and
assistant to the chancellor, responded to Rosa's e-mail inspection request with the following letter:

> *Dear Ms. Fuller:*
> *...After careful consideration, we believe that the mate-*
> *rials you have requested are either not public records or are*
> *protected from disclosure by the personnel records exception*
> *to the Public Records Act or by the federal Family*
> *Educational Rights and Privacy Act.*
>
> *Not every e-mail sent or received over the campus com-*
> *puting network is a public record of the State of North*
> *Carolina. The Public Records Act of the State of North*
> *Carolina...defines a public record as being, made "pursuant*
> *to law or ordinance in connection with the transaction of*
> *public business" by an agency or officer of the State. While*
> *Dr. Adams is an employee of the State, it is apparent from*
> *the face of the document that you provided us that the e-*
> *mail you are concerned about is an expression of personal*
> *opinion in connection with a general public discourse.*
> *UNCW's Computing Resource Use Policy...expressly per-*
> *mits occasional personal use of the computer network by fac-*
> *ulty, staff, and students where not in conflict with the dom-*

inant purposes for which the network was established. The policy specifically "recognizes the value and potential of publishing on the Internet, and so allows and encourages students, staff, and faculty to do so consistent with this policy."

We are sensitive to the concerns that you expressed in your letter regarding the communication from Dr. Adams that you provided. However, the question of whether or not Dr. Adams' discourse was appropriate in tone or content is a personnel and computer usage issue that is considered in a different context, both in terms of university policies and also in terms of the First Amendment. However, in the context of a public records request, it is clear from the communication that you provided that Dr. Adams was not speaking in his official role as a faculty member, but rather as an individual member of the university community...

Hal White

October 1, 2001:
Rosa responded to Mr. White with the following message:

...You state, in your response, your opinion that these e-mail messages "are either not public records or are protected from disclosure by the personnel records exception to the Public Records Act or by the federal Family Educational Rights and Privacy Act." I believe these records are public records and are not protected by either Act you cite.

1. You cite the Public Records Act, which defines a public record as "all documents, papers, letters," etc., "regardless of physical form or characteristics, made or received pursuant to law or ordinance in connection with the transaction of public business by any agency of North Carolina govern-

ment or its subdivisions." This would seem to include any and every e-mail sent by an employee of the University, from a University e-mail address, with the use of the University's central computing facilities and services. But you claim that Adams, while "an employee of the State," sent me an abusive e-mail message as "an expression of personal opinion in connection with a general public discourse." This claim ignores the fact that Adams sent me his e-mail letter in response to the e-mail letter I sent him, dated 15 September 2001, which I addressed "To the students and faculty of the University of North Carolina at Wilmington." I addressed him as a faculty member. I had a course with him last year. He well knew he had received this letter from a student. (A note: Adams explicitly refused in his message to participate in a public discourse. He instead reviled me with a series of abusive epithets. He offered no evidence and no argument in support of these abusive names. Name-calling is the nullification of discourse.) You conclude that Adams, in his e-mail letter to me, "was not speaking in his official role as a faculty member," and was "not transacting public business on behalf of the State of North Carolina." Your definition of the "official role" and "Public business" of a University faculty member is arbitrary, tendentious and unduly narrow...

2. You cite "UNCW's Computing Resource Use Policy [which] expressly permits occasional personal use of the computer network by faculty, staff, and students where not in conflict with the dominant purposes for which the network was established." But this policy also states that such "occasional, brief personal uses are permissible" if and only if this "use does not harm or invade the rights of others." I believe I have a right, as a student at this University, not to be sent abusive e-mail messages, by a member of the faculty...

3. You further cite the University's Computing Resource Use Policy, which "recognizes the value and potential of publishing on the Internet, and so allows and encourages students, staff, and faculty to do so consistent with this policy." Adams' abusive letter is hardly "publishing on the Internet" in the sense clearly intended in the policy. An e-mail letter is not a "personal page." Furthermore, his letter is inconsistent with the policy, inasmuch as it harms my right not to receive such abusive communications...

4. You claim the e-mail messages I wish to inspect are "protected from disclosure by the personnel records exception to the Public Records Act." This claim is false. I have not asked to see any personnel records.

5. You also claim the e-mail messages I wish to inspect are protected from disclosure "by the federal Family Educational Rights and Privacy Act." This claim is false. FERPA has to do with the privacy of education records. I have not asked to see any education records.

6. You claim the e-mail messages I wish to inspect "are personal, and thus the property of a private person as set forth in GS 132-1.2 (2)." This section of the Public Records Act is irrelevant to your claim. It has only to do with "trade secrets." I have not asked to see any trade secrets.

Your opinion in this case is based on irrelevant laws, misinterpreted policies, and arbitrary definitions. Therefore, I continue to ask the Office of Information Technology, and any other appropriate office or officer, to let me and my representatives inspect the e-mail messages Mike Adams sent, with the use of the University's central computing facilities and services...from September 15 to September 18...

October 3, 2001:

By this time, Chancellor Leutze had instructed Hal White to ignore Fuller's increasingly hostile and sarcastic requests. Nonetheless, he responded with a letter that prompted Fuller to make another request on October 10th. White responded yet again on October 11th. The increasingly hostile exchanges ended with a letter by Fuller threatening a lawsuit in mid-October.

October 15, 2001:

Mr. White:

I understand that the "decision of the University," as you put it in your October 11 letter, "is final." I understand you believe "it serves no further purpose to continue a debate about the decision." I also have no wish to debate this decision further in letters between us. What I don't understand is this: what is the University's decision?

You write that the University is "not prepared to force Dr. Adams to produce all the e-mail to and from his campus e-mail address between the dates of September 15 and September 18, 2001." Should I understand this to be the University's final decision"?

I have never asked the University to let me see the e-mail messages sent to Mike Adams at his University e-mail address.

I have never asked the University to force Mike Adams to let me see his e-mail correspondence. I have asked the University to let me see the e-mail messages sent by him from his e-mail address on and between the said dates. I under-stand the University already has these messages in its custody and under its control. Dr. Robert Tyndall has assured me the University will, in accordance with your directive, do what is in its "power to ensure that the e-mail records under discussion are preserved." The University could hardly preserve these messages if Adams alone had them in his custody and under his control.

I also have not asked the University to let me see all the e-mail messages sent by Mike Adams from September 15 to September 18, if some of those messages contain any personnel records or personally identifiable student records. I have asked the University to separate the confidential from the non-confidential information in these messages.

The University's "final decision" as you put it, is then evidently this: it will not do what I have not asked it to do. Why would the University decide not to do what I have not asked it to do? Is this really supposed to be the University's "final decision"? This odd, if not entirely novel, decision seems to be the result of an insufficiently intimate familiarity with the canons of logic.

I suspect that the University has decided not to do what I have not asked it to do because a decision not to do what I really have asked it to do would put it in open defiance of State law...

If the University refuses to do an inventory of the e-mail letters Mike Adams sent on the relevant dates, or refuses to let me see his "official" messages, other than the ones exempt under the law, then it stands in open and absolute defiance of State law. The matter will then have to be finally decided in another forum...

The provost then called to tell me that they had some good news and some bad news. The good news was that Rosa was not requesting all of my e-mails anymore. The bad news was that the university would have to "work with me" to sort through my account and determine what was and was not a public record. I was told to call Hal White for a more detailed explanation of the requirements of the law.

When I called Hal, I was immediately impressed with his sense of humor and his general good nature. We talked about politics, the tragedy of 9/11, and, of course, the direction that the e-mail controversy was heading. After about an hour of conversation, Hal told me that he would be heading to my office later in the week with a member of the Information Technology Systems Division (ITSD), to look at my office computer to see if there were any messages sent between September 15 to September 18 in either the outbox or the trash bin of my e-mail account.

While objecting to the proposed inspection of my computer, I wasn't that outraged until White and the ITSD officer, Ellen Gurganious, arrived in my office. The look on both of their faces is etched in my memory. It was certainly an awkward moment for everyone involved. They found no messages between the dates in question either in my outbox or my trash bin. Those messages had all been deleted before White told me to start preserving my messages on October 10. Before they left the office, I looked at both White and Gurganious and said, "I know you can't comment on what I have to say, but this is a truly psychotic act of retaliation over nothing more than a petty difference of political opinion." They both agreed and White apologized for the intrusion. He knew it was an unacceptable invasion of privacy. Indeed, White had told me previously on the telephone that the whole thing was, in his opinion, an act of retaliation and political harassment. Nonetheless, Rosa had threatened to sue and UNCW's involvement in the dispute was far from over.

Krysten and a professor named Donna King were the only people on campus that ITSD had identified as having received messages from me between September 15 and September 18.

Hal White contacted both of them to let them know that the university would be checking its backup tapes and eventually reading the messages I sent them in order to determine if they were public records to be turned over to Rosa and her family. Both objected to the investigation of the e-mail accounts. But Krysten was a little more vocal in her objections.

In addition to e-mailing Thor Halvorssen, she called our friend and attorney Charlton Allen, who advised her to demand that the investigation be stopped and, if unsuccessful, to demand to be present if any of the messages sent to her account were opened. White expressed distaste for the word "demand" but conceded to her "request" to be present for the inspection of our correspondence. King did not request to be present for the opening of the e-mails as my only e-mail to her was a course scheduling request that she had deleted immediately. In fact, it was eventually found that since it was deleted so quickly, its contents did not end up on the backup tapes.

After a couple of e-mail exchanges with Mike Sheehan at ITSD, an appointment was scheduled for him to meet Hal White, Krysten, and me at an ITSD office in Hoggard Hall to open and read e-mails for the purpose of determining whether they were, a) private correspondence or, b) public records to be turned over to Fuller and her parents. Although they had received some negative press from the *Washington Times* and radio talk show host Neal Boortz, it looked like Rosa and her family had prevailed on the ultimate issue. Meanwhile, Charlton Allen was working on an article that would turn this investigation into a national news item.

The Enemy in Our Midst

October 25, 2001:

At about 11 a.m., I walked into Mike Sheehan's office across campus in Hoggard Hall. There I met Hal White and Krysten for the forced opening of our private e-mail correspondence. Sheehan stated his objections to the procedure before we began by saying, "This wasn't my decision" and "I get no pleasure out of what is happening here today."

When he pulled up the two messages from me to Krysten that had been preserved on the back-up tapes, White read enough of the messages to determine that they were not public records but, instead, private correspondence. After reading the messages, he wrote a letter to Rosa, explaining how it was impossible for our communications to be public records. Nonetheless, we had gone through this ordeal feeling like two characters in a Kafka novel. On our way out of the building,

Krysten said that she felt like she was living in communist China. She was outraged over what seemed like a clear victory for Rosa, which would never have happened if her mother was not a professor and administrator at UNCW.

Furthermore, this intrusion occurred in Krysten's workplace just a few steps down the hall from the office where she worked. Many of her co-workers looked at her suspiciously after learning that her account was being examined, wondering exactly what she had done wrong.

When I arrived back in my office around 11:30, my inbox was flooded with scores of e-mails. I immediately remembered a meeting I recently had with Charlton Allen, where he proposed writing an editorial about the e-mail controversy for David Horowitz's Internet Web magazine, called *Front Page*. When I logged on to *www.frontpagemag.com*, I saw the following headline and read the article that was generating all the e-mails I got that morning:

Rampant Anti-Americanism surfaces at the University of North Carolina at Wilmington
By Charlton L. Allen

The University of North Carolina at Wilmington (UNCW) is not known as a hotbed of campus liberalism—but don't blame Dr. Patti Turrisi, or her daughter Rosa Fuller. After the vicious terrorist attacks of September 11th, most of America came together with a unity of purpose unseen since World War II. But not this mother-daughter team.

Immediately after the terrorist attacks, Rosa sent out an unsolicited e-mail entitled "In Dedication to An Undivided Humanity" to a number of people affiliated with UNCW. This e-mail was the usual diatribe against America, assigning blame for the attacks not to the hijackers, not to Osama Bin Laden, not to the Taliban, but instead blaming the usual militant left scapegoats of the Reagan-Bush administration, US-Israeli policy, "petty bourgeois squabbling," etc. The only source cited in the e-mail for the numerous lies, distortions, and fabrications presented as fact was the World Socialist Web site. Nothing more need be said.

One of the recipients of Rosa's tirade was Dr. Mike Adams, a professor in the UNCW criminal justice department. A proud patriot, Dr. Adams was incensed. He responded to Rosa and forwarded his response to a number of people in his address book, just as Rosa requested in her initial e-mail. Specifically, Dr. Adams stated that, while Rosa was entitled to enunciate her views, they were wholly undeserving of serious consideration, not to mention intentionally divisive, despite Rosa's self-proclaimed "dedication."

Dr. Adams' simple act of proffering his contrarian view infuriated Rosa and her mother, the aforementioned Turrisi. Their reaction was typical of the militant left when confronted with their own hypocrisy: they attempted to silence the opinions of those who disagree, not unlike the Taliban.

First, when Rosa received negative feedback from individuals who received Dr. Adams' forwarded e-mail, she attempted to file charges with the University Police Department, claiming that the often-heated responses created a "hostile environment" that rose to the level of communicating threats. Realizing that Rosa's claim was frivolous, the University Police declined to press charges, but not before calling numerous students in for questioning. Further, parents of these students received phone calls from the authorities indicating their children were wanted for intimidating a fellow student.

Rosa, with the likely coaching of her mother, then lodged a complaint with the university administration, demanding that the University allow her and her representatives access to all e-mail messages sent by Dr. Adams for a four-day period in September, implying that, because he called her unintelligent and divisive, Adams had somehow defamed and intimidated her. Again, the uni-

versity rejected her claims. This was not surprising, since there was no legal basis for her complaint in the first place.

Frustrated, but undeterred, Turrisi and daughter have contacted the chair of Dr. Adams' department and demanded a full investigation of Dr. Adams, in addition to their insistence that the university forward Dr. Adams' e-mails. Again, the university denied their claims. Turrisi maintains that it is her intention to file a lawsuit for defamation and, pursuant to the Freedom of Information Act, to seek access to Dr. Adams' correspondence.

"I have not threatened anyone, nor have I attempted to silence anyone who disagrees with me on these issues," Dr. Adams said. "But if Dr. Turrisi continues to lead this witch hunt, I'll have my mother call her department chair."

Turrisi appears to have quite a history of filing frivolous complaints based upon her warped political ideals. According to a source with the university, several years ago, she demanded the university discipline a colleague who disagreed with her regarding the general statutory principle for several degrees of rape, a rule followed by all Jurisdictions in the United States. Apparently, Turrisi believes that a professor who argues that some rapes are worse than others is unfit to teach America's youth.

The point, perhaps lost upon Rosa and Turrisi, is that their efforts to silence others with whom they disagree are exactly the methods they accuse Dr. Adams and others of using: namely, intimidation and intolerance. They illustrate that not all sanctimonious hypocrites are hiding in the caves of Afghanistan.

I had warned the provost that if Dr. Turrisi didn't back off, I would call out the big guns. I also promised Hal White that the public relations consequences of reading my e-mail would be severe. Now, everything was clearly starting to unfold. Allen's article was about to catch the attention of *US News and World Report*, and, eventually, Sean Hannity.

Before I get ahead of myself, Hal White had to send the following letter to Rosa and her father explaining that they would not be getting copies of any of the e-mails that they had already examined. The university would, however, give them other records concerning my e-mail communications. The administration would later be accused of trying to cover it up:

Dear Ms Fuller,

...In response to your request, I asked the Information Technology Systems Division, System Programming Section, to undertake a review of the transmittal logs of the back-up tapes from the dates September 15-September 18. These tapes were retained in response to your request of September 28 that the University take reasonable steps to preserve the records you had requested...Those logs revealed 23 e-mails from the address adamsm@uncwil.edu during the dates in question, all of them on September 17 and 18. A list of these e-mails and the addresses to which they were sent are attached.

I also asked ITSD to look in the actual file boxes of the back-up tapes to retrieve as many of the subject mails as possible in order to ascertain their status as public records or not, according to the criteria set forth in my earlier letters to you...As it turned out, none of Dr. Adams' outgoing mail was captured by our system backups. Therefore, next we decided to look in the in-boxes on our central computing facility (VAX) of the on-campus recipients of that mail to see if it still resided there. As you will see from the attached list, there were only two on-campus recipients, kingd@uncwil.edu (faculty) and scottk@uncwil.edu (student). We then notified the recipients that we were going to inspect any e-mails residing in their in-boxes that were transmitted from adamsm@uncwil.edu on any of the specified dates. Needless to say, this caused predictable consternation, outrage, and a feeling of violation and invasion of privacy on the part of those whose mail was to be inspected. While it is certainly true that access to the system comes with only a conditional expectation of privacy, both our student and our faculty member felt they were being coerced and "forced," even if your series of requests did not use such terms. Nevertheless, because your request was properly defined and limited, and because there was no other way to ascertain the categories of mail without looking at them, we indicated that we would, and then we did examine their in-boxes over their objections pursuant to your request.

Unfortunately, Dr. King's in-box did not have the e-mail from Dr. Adams. Apparently, and from discussion with her, she apparently disposed of it upon reading it--a common practice. Both Dr. King and Dr. Adams indicate it was a brief memo concerning the scheduling of classes next semester. We then examined the in-box of the student. Of the seven e-mails sent to the student's address during the defined period, only two remained on the VAX logs...After examination of the two remaining e-mails in the student's in-box, it was very clear that the mail was personal and private, and not a public record. The student is not now, nor has she ever been, in Dr. Adams' class or one of his advisees, and the mail did not discuss academic matters or matters of student life. Therefore, this mail will not be produced.

Having failed to retrieve all the sent mail during the defined period from the VAX logs, we asked Dr. Adams, Dr. King, and the student to examine the logs on their personal PCs. You can imagine how welcome that request was. Of course, we informed the student that a private, student-owned PC is not subject to coerced inspection, and that thus the student was not required to comply with our request. The student *refused to allow us to inspect her PC. As to the two professors, although the office PC is usually treated by the university as if private in most regards, for example, in regard to the copyright of articles and books written on it, as well as for the incidental personal use exception, we nevertheless informed the professors that in our opinion they were required to let us inspect their computer logs if we felt it to be necessary. Both indicated that we must do so over their objection, and that they do not archive sent mail. Dr. King also indicated that she did not save the scheduling memo from Dr. Adams on her PC. The inspection of Dr. Adams's PC revealed that he had not archived the sent mails and that there were no other files or folders in which they resided. Naturally, we are unable to retrieve sent mail from any of the seven off-campus addresses that are listed, one of which appears to be a family address in any case.*

These are the results of our efforts to comply with your request…

October 26, 2001:

I got a call at about 5 p.m. from Thor Halvorssen insisting that I call John Leo at *US News & World Report*. Leo had told Thor that the administration was denying that it read any of my private e-mail correspondence. When I called Leo, he asked only one question; "Did the university read your e-mail?" When I told him they did, he simply said "Thanks. I like what you're doing down there, and I'm going to write about it."

October 29, 2001:

I went to Barnes & Noble to pick up a copy of Leo's column in *US News & World Report*. The same day Leo's article came out, Rosa accused me of libel with the following complaint to the university:

I said, in my September 20 complaint, "If it is found that [Mike] Adams sent his false representation of me to others, inside or outside the University community, and if these others acted on his false representation, and sent me abusive e-mail messages, then I also shall accuse him of libel" in violation of the University's Computing Resource Use Policy. I now have evidence that Adams did send his false representation of me to both University and non-University people.

1. *Adams caused his attorney, Charlton L. Allen, to publish a false and libelous article in an Internet magazine, Front Page, on October 25 (FrontPageMagazine.com). This article states that Adams "responded to Rosa and forwarded his response to a number of people in his address book, just as Rosa requested in her initial e-mail." I never asked Adams to forward his response. I stated this conditional: "If you support open, unbiased, democratic discussion of all the facts, please forward this e-mail to friends and acquaintances both on and off campus." I asked him to forward my statement, if and only if he supported an "open, unbiased, democratic discussion of all the facts." Adams' letter to me proves he has no interest in such a discussion. He therefore had no right to forward my e-mail to anyone. He received my statement in his role as a faculty member. When he forwarded my statement, he violated POLICY G, "Joint Statement on Rights and Freedoms of Students," which states: "Information about student views, beliefs and political associations which professors acquire in the course of their work as instructors, advisors, and counselors should be considered confidential. Protection against improper disclosure is a serious professional obligation."*

2. *Adams also mocked the fact that, after I received e-mail threats from people in his "address book," my mother contacted his department chair, and asked him to (1) find out what Adams had sent these people and (2) persuade Adams to help us stop these threats. Adams' attorney quotes him as having said: "But if Dr. Turrisi continues to lead this witch hunt, I'll have my mother call her department chair." This statement indicates that Adams has no sense of the difference in status between a faculty member and a student.*

3. *The University Counsel provided me with a list of the nine e-mail messages sent by Adams (ADAMSM) to UNCW addresses on September 17 and September 18. This list shows that, on September 17, Adams sent a UNCW student, Krysten Scott (SCOTTK), three e-mail messages (at 9:03 a.m., 9:06 a.m., and 9:11 a.m.) shortly before she sent me an abusive, profane and threatening e-mail message (at 9:38 a.m.) Adams sent me his abusive e-mail letter at 9:45 a.m. He then sent Scott three more e-mail messages on this date (at 9:57 a.m., 9:59 a.m., and at 12:33 p.m.) This evidence indicates that Adams forwarded my statement as well as his false representation of me to Scott. She acted on his false representation and sent me an abusive and threatening e-mail communication.*

I, therefore, accuse Mike Adams of libel in violation of the University's Computing Resource Use Policy. I ask the University to investigate my allegation and, if warranted, hold Adams accountable for his conduct under all applicable University policies and procedures.

Rosa T. Fuller

November 1, 2001:

Rosa's dad (Dennis Fuller) wrote an op/ed article to the UNCW student newspaper criticizing me as well as the paper for its previous article about the controversy, saying, "The Seahawk, in its news article and a column by its editor, obscures the fact that this professor tried to stifle the free speech of this student (Rosa)." He went on to say that I "offered no defense of US policies or actions, past or present" and "instead berated (Rosa) with a series of abusive names, which falsely represented her as 'dishonest,' 'bigoted,' 'unintelligent' and 'immature.'... (with) no argument in support of these abusive names" and that I "sent (my) inflammatory misrepresentation of Rosa to several people" and that Rosa "received abusive, threatening, profane and libelous e-mail messages from many of them ..."

Dennis went on to include information in his op/ed about my e-mail communications, including the times of the communications and names of the people I had contacted. He seemed utterly unaware that the problem he and his family were facing was that most people thought they were, at best, "thought" police, or, at worst, just plain nuts.

I admit that I could have clarified things by joining in and telling Dennis that I didn't forward any copies of my response until well after I was accused of "berating her" (that was several weeks later, by the way), but I thought it would be more fun to let Dennis make that claim as a way of rationalizing the hostile responses to Rosa's "dedication." Indeed, what seemed lost on the Turrisi-Fuller family was the possibility that people were mad at Rosa, not because I told them to be mad, but because her constitutionally protected e-mail was also illtimed and intentionally provocative. I guess they don't make communists like they used to.

November 2, 2001:

At about 5 p.m., I got a message from the Fox News show, Hannity & Colmes, wanting me to appear on national TV to discuss the e-mail controversy. Since they said they were going to invite the other side (Rosa, or perhaps Dennis), I knew I could not turn them down. Before the appearance, FIRE's director of Legal and Public Advocacy, Greg Lukianoff, penned the following letter to the chancellor.

November 8, 2001:

    Dear Chancellor Leutze:

    ...We are profoundly distressed by the threat to free speech and privacy posed by the administration's handling of the baseless claims of university student Rosa Fuller. It is doubly offensive that the University of North Carolina at Wilmington's capitulation in the face of Fuller's unreasonable demands came after the school had shown its determination to protect the speech and privacy rights of its faculty and students. In this time of national crisis, it is more important than ever that we affirm our cherished Constitution and not abandon freedom, even when faced with the possibility of litigation.

    ...After a painstaking back and forth with University Counsel and escalating threats by Fuller, the University decided to examine Professor Adams' e-mails, over his vocal objection, in fulfillment of Fuller's request.

    ...The outrageousness of this invasion should be self-evident. Even by her own evidence, Rosa Fuller has no legitimate legal claim on the basis of intimidation, defamation, false representation, or threats. Even if she did have some sort of claim, UNCW should have shown the courage necessary to protect its faculty's freedom of speech and privacy. Instead of

rightly refusing any of Fuller's requests, UNCW has legitimized Fuller's frivolous and dangerous legal claims.

Fuller's claimed right to access Adams' e-mails as "public records" cannot be taken seriously and is a perversion of the law that should not have been entertained by University Counsel. More importantly, since she was using dubious legal argument in an attempt to punish students and faculty for exercising their Free Speech rights, her request should have been rejected out of hand.

...Now UNCW has ominously demonstrated that when the most basic rights of students and faculty are threatened, UNCW is not above abandoning them. The chill that this will send into every communication on your campus is palpable.

Perhaps the deepest irony is that UNCW has not insulated itself from this or any other litigation. Instead, it has opened the floodgates to litigation by anyone who objects to the failure of their arguments in open discourse. It is a frightening and dangerous precedent.

As you know full well, UNCW is a public university and therefore has an overarching legal obligation, in addition to its moral obligation, to ensure the privacy and First Amendment rights of its faculty and students. Even if no formal retaliation ever takes place against the accused students or Professor Adams, the mere threat of action promotes self-censorship among faculty and students alike, chilling both protected speech and academic freedom. This, of course, runs completely contrary to the role and constitutional obligations of a great university. As should be clear, a university in which students and faculty have any fear of reprisal for discussing controversial topics is one that is rendered impotent to address society's most crucial issues.

Accordingly, FIRE requests that you and your adminis-

tration:

1) *Affirm to Professor Adams that he has committed no wrong by either disagreeing with Fuller or by circulating her own, unaltered words.*

2) *Apologize in appropriate terms to Professor Adams for this invasion of his privacy and state unequivocally that UNCW will not violate the privacy rights of students and faculty.*

3) *Reject Rosa Fuller's claims as contrivances intended to punish students and faculty for the exercise of their First Amendment rights.*

4) *Permit no further university retaliation against students or faculty for their disagreement with any person's views, in the interest of full and robust discourse, and in fulfillment of your constitutional and moral obligations.*

Before signing off, Lukianoff urged the chancellor to log on to www.thefire.org to see what happens when universities ignore FIRE's requests. Before the end of the semester, they would deeply regret their decision to ignore that warning.

November 9, 2001:

I was a little nervous about the prospect of appearing in front of millions of TV viewers to discuss the e-mail controversy, especially after someone put flyers up all over campus telling the time and station of the appearance. Many students had become regular viewers of Fox News in the wake of September 11th and I knew that the millions of viewers would include scores (if not hundreds) of UNCW students and faculty. When I finally arrived at the studio in Raleigh and was wired to the New York studio, I heard a familiar voice introducing my segment:

COLMES: Welcome back to Hannity & Colmes. I'm Allen Colmes.

After the terror attacks of September 11th, a University of North Carolina student sent out an e-mail blaming the US for the attacks on its own soil. One of the recipients was criminal justice Professor Mike Adams, who responded to the student, calling her missive immature and divisive. And now the writer says she's gotten threatening e-mails from other students and blames Adams for inciting violence against her. Have the terrorist attacks affected the right of free speech? Joining us from Raleigh, North Carolina, Professor Mike Adams. Mike, I may not always be on your side politically, but I think you're absolutely right in this case. Tell us your story.

ADAMS: Well, we're never on the side—same side politically probably, but I was impressed with the way you handled Malik Shabazz last week.

COLMES: Thank you, sir. Go ahead. Let's hear what happened.

ADAMS: But what happened was that I was sent this inflammatory e-mail message, as you said, blaming the attacks on the United States of America, calling Bush an illegitimate president, and I responded simply implying— strongly implying—it was a bigoted, immature, and unintelligent speech. I basically forwarded the message to some other people because she asked me to do that.

COLMES: Well, she sent out this mass e-mail. First of all, I'm tired of all of these mass e-mails. If you want to write to me, I love getting e-mail. But write to me. Don't send me mass e-mails. And then you're accused—how dare you take this and send it to other people when they ask you to, and you did not call her immature. You said her interest—you said the—her conv—her speech perhaps was immature in this case. You didn't call her names. You said the claimed interest in promoting rational discussion was dishonest. You didn't call her those names. You qualified it.

ADAMS: Right. Exactly. And it's just amazing, just the audacity of threatening to sue me for defamation of character, and just the ridiculous request for the university to turn over a whole week's worth of my e-mail to look through and suggest that I incited some kind of violence for...

COLMES: Now this is really the part I find extremely troubling. The university...

ADAMS: It is troubling.

COLMES:...went and got permission—what, legally they were able to get your e-mail and—get to it?

ADAMS: Well, they were, you know, very good at first, and they recognized that first request as being absurd and being too broad and, basically after that, she narrowed the request asking them to comb through my e-mail and see if there were anything—there was anything that fell under a public records exception. That required reading a couple of my personal e-mails, and I have a bit of a problem with that.

HANNITY: Well, you should have a big problem with that. Welcome to the show. Sean Hannity here.

ADAMS: Thank you, Sean.

HANNITY: You did—look, you did a thousand percent the right thing here, and—I just want to go through this a little bit here because she accused the United States of being an imperial—being involved in imperialist warfare. She quotes a socialist Web site in particular. All you said is the Constitution protects bigoted, unintelligent, and immature speech. I thought that was very well written on your part.

ADAMS: That's right. Well, thanks. And, you know, it's just an obvious response. It was a very tamed response. You know, I considered writing something a lot more hostile than that, but I took my time and thought before I wrote. I regret I didn't unload on her now.

HANNITY: No, and I—I've—that's wise. I think that's smart. Well, it said at the end of the e-mail to forward it.

ADAMS: You know what's interesting. I forwarded it to— forwarded that to fewer people than she initially wrote it to and, of course, everyone's forwarding it to everyone and, all of a sudden, you know, people started to say some silly things and they went a little overboard, I suppose, but God knows where they got it from. It's all over the place because you assume the risk when you hit the send button.

HANNITY: Right. You hit that send button, and you want people—and you would think on a piece—particularly one like this that was meant to be provocative...

ADAMS: It was just attention seeking and, you know, you assume the risk and, you know, this is all about taking responsibility for your own actions, and that's something we have to start teaching at the university to a much greater degree. You're responsible for your own conduct, and you assume the risk. When you join in, you know, in the marketplace of ideas, you better expect that there's a good chance someone's going to fire back at you...

HANNITY:...So this all comes down, and you're accused of—what was it specifically?

ADAMS: I guess conspiring to hurt someone's feelings or something like that. I can't figure it out. You know, defamation of character was not something she ever had a chance of winning a cause of action for, so combing through my e-mail account, you know, I guess to find evidence for that, I think, was highly suspect, and I think—you know, this was an intrusion, but I think it raises a larger question, and here's the question I have. If I were a feminist professor and

I had offended a male student, is there any chance that the man could have said, "You hurt my feelings. Let me into that feminist professor's e-mail account." It's never happened before, and I doubt it would ever happen.

HANNITY: Well, that's a serious issue here. What are you planning to do with this?

ADAMS: What am I planning to do? Well, I guess...

HANNITY: You could always get the ACLU to back you.

ADAMS: Well, I don't know about that. I'm not going to stoop that low quite frankly.

COLMES: Oh, come on.

ADAMS: Sorry about that, Alan. I had to take a shot at you, but—at any rate, no. I'm just going to sit back and answer questions and tell the truth, because I think someone needs to expose this because this exerts...

HANNITY: Right. Are you going...

ADAMS: ...a serious chilling effect on free speech, and that needs to be stopped.

HANNITY: I totally agree with you, and they didn't have a right to do it, and—especially here. Now are you—is there any threat of a lawsuit? I read a letter that her father had—I believe it was her father...

ADAMS: Oh, her father? Well, that's interesting.

HANNITY: Well...

ADAMS: Well, she claimed in her original letter we live in a racist and chauvinist society. Why is daddy speaking for her? That's another question.

HANNITY: She said, "Well, we have no intentions of suing for libel. We think it's absurd, but"—they think you're acting like a martyr and, quote, "He's an unsavory character."

ADAMS: An unsavory character.

HANNITY: That's from Dennis Fuller.

ADAMS: Well, that means conservative, so—at least I don't

log on to the world socialist Web sites.

COLMES: Oh, don't talk about conservatives like that, Mike. Come on. Look, I think you've got a beef—a real beef with the university in terms of them wanting to expose your e-mail. I find that extremely troubling. Are you pursuing anything in terms of legal action?

ADAMS: Oh, no. I have no intention of doing that at all.

COLMES: Why not?

ADAMS: Why not? Well, I'm not a litigious person. I prefer to fight my battles in the court of public opinion, and here I am.

COLMES: It doesn't seem to bother you that much. I mean, I think that's an incredible invasion of privacy, and I bet the ACLU would probably, indeed, be willing to get involved in something like that.

ADAMS: It does bother me, but if this brings about a change and it never happens again, that would be reward enough, I suppose, so...

COLMES: So what's the status now? What's—what's going to happen next?

ADAMS: I'm not sure. You know, I guess—it would be nice if the other side—you know, if this family would stop trying to win this battle in the court of public opinion. They just keep getting slaughtered, I think, but if they want to keep going, I'll go another round.

COLMES: Well, we invited Ms. Fuller to be on tonight. We were told that she had some surgery, could not be with us. We certainly would like to hear her side.

ADAMS: Well, I'm available to come back.

COLMES: I'm not sure that I disagree with everything she's written probably as much as you do. I mean, she talked about we have to examine our motives, look at America. In this country, if you talk about even looking at America and critically examining it, you get called anti-American and a traitor, and people act—react emotionally to that.

ADAMS: Well, I never did that, and I didn't react emotionally, and I just point you to one line in my response. I said, you know, you have a constitutional right to say the things that you said, and so I've never lost sight of that principle.

COLMES: Well, that's why I'm on your side in this case because you pointed out that she has—you have a constitutional right to be immature, to say something that you may think is not as intelligent as something else somebody says, so …

ADAMS: Absolutely.

COLMES: We thank you very much...

After they unhooked my microphone, it took a few minutes for it to sink in that liberal Alan Colmes and conservative Sean Hannity had actually both taken my side during the segment. As I enjoyed the ride home, I wondered what kind of surgery Rosa was recovering from. Perhaps it was an ego reduction.

Author's Note: In a recent article, I jokingly referred to Hannity & Colmes as the "Hannity" show, claiming that I couldn't remember Alan's name. I was just kidding. That was actually a cheap attempt to get back on the show. Furthermore, I was wrong to tell Alan that we never agreed on anything politically. Aside from the issue that brought me on his show, I have actually agreed with Alan twice. On all other occasions he has been wrong.

Where There's Smoke, There's Fire

December 3, 2001:

In November, Rosa's father had actually asked the FIRE to abandon its support of me in favor of his daughter. While his letter is too long to reproduce, the reply from FIRE's Greg Lukianoff should be required reading for students and administrators at every public university:

> *Dear Dr. (Dennis) Fuller,*
>
> *...In your letter of November 26, you said that if we could point to any core political speech in the response of Dr. Adams, Krysten Scott, James Ryan, or Edward Wagensellar, then your daughter "would retract all her accusations and send each one of these people and the University an apology." Virtually all the content of each of their responses is, in fact, considered political speech (the*

"core" is routinely added in Constitutional law to emphasize that political speech is the type of speech that we, as a society, consider most important). Irrespective of whether or not these remarks are crude or dismissive, they express a clear political opinion in opposition to your daughter's political opinion. Furthermore, in disagreeing, her critics offered other political opinions, including Krysten Scott's statement: "I do not agree with anyone who gives Muslims in our country a hard time. They are hard working Americans who don't deserve this." I am at a loss to understand how that isn't political speech.

I believe the confusion comes from your repeated assertion that Dr. Adams's speech is somehow invalid, because he did not specifically engage and refute her ideas in a "rational discussion." Free speech is not limited by your ideas of politeness, decorum, or the proper way to argue, and certainly not by some arbitrary definition of "rationality"—nor should it be. To allow anyone to dismiss free speech rights on the basis of your criteria would utterly destroy free speech and leave it entirely in the hands of the arbiters of "propriety." I strongly encourage you to read the landmark Supreme Court cases Cohen v. California 403 US 15 (1971) and Hustler Magazine, Inc. et al. v. Jerry Falwell, 485 US 46 (1988). These cases protect, as core political speech, highly offensive material, dismissive phrases, farce, profanity, and exaggeration that make the worst of the responses to your daughter look like polite tearoom chatter. A further examination of Constitutional law will demonstrate to you the undeniable truth that virtually all of the responses you referenced are considered political speech. In the eyes of the Constitution, the speech of your daughter and the speech of her critics are equally valid. I hope this demonstrates to you why it is so important to resist any attempt to punish Dr.

Adams and other individuals who responded. I am confident that you will follow through on your promise and that your daughter will apologize to Dr. Adams, Krysten Scott, James Ryan, Edward Wagensellar, and the University, so that this matter can finally be put to rest.

...If you are still interested in some of the legal issues remaining in this case, please look into the legal definitions of "threat," "defamation," and "false representation." The fact that all of the criticisms pointed to were entirely subjective, hyperbolic, or conveyed no direct and imminent harm by the author keeps them well within the range of perfectly legal political criticism.

I think you would be surprised at the range of speech that the Supreme Court has deemed to be protected. In Terminiello v. Chicago, *337 US 1 (1949), the Court reversed a disturbing-the-peace conviction of a notorious racist and anti-Semite. Justice Douglas wrote that speech is protected even when its purpose is to "induce a condition of unrest, create dissatisfaction with conditions as they are, or even stir people to anger." In an important civil rights case,* Gooding v. Wilson, *405 US 518 (1972), the Court reversed the conviction of a citizen who called a police officer a "white son of a bitch" and added "I'll kill you." The vote to reverse was 5-2. In* Papish v. Board of Curators of the University of Missouri, *410 US 667 (1973), the Court ordered the reinstatement of a journalism student who had distributed a cartoon depicting policemen raping the Statue of Liberty and the Goddess of Justice.* **The Court held that "conventions of decency" did not dictate what speech was protected on a public college campus.** *I urge you to read the seminal opinion in* Brandenburg v. Ohio, *395 US 444 (1969), which limited restriction of speech to "advocacy (that) is directed to inciting or producing immi-*

nent lawless action and is likely to incite or produce such action." That case involved members of the Ku Klux Klan, suggesting that violence against blacks and Jews might be appropriate to protect "white Christian society." Thus, the mere advocacy of violence was protected, as long as the speaker took no steps to implement it. In Sweezy v. New Hampshire, 354 US 234 (1957), a professor at a state university, a self-styled "classical Marxist" and "socialist," was deemed to have uttered protected speech when he criticized the use of violence by capitalist nations seeking to preserve a social order that he felt should, and would, eventually collapse. This collapse, predicted Prof. Paul Sweezy approvingly, would be met by violence on the part of those seeking to create a "truly human society," namely the socialists. The legislature of New Hampshire had sought to suppress what it deemed to be advocacy of violence, but the Supreme Court protected such advocacy. Given what you describe your daughter's political views to be, she, too, should read Sweezy, and she should be proud and grateful to live in a free society that allows people like Professor Sweezy to air their political views without punishment or censorship. It is one of the crowning glories of our constitutional system. Neither you nor your daughter would want to see the Sweezy opinion either overturned or ignored on college campuses of higher education. Today it protects Professor Adams; tomorrow your daughter might have to seek its protection. The First Amendment, happily, is there for all of us. This is what FIRE is all about...

> *Greg Lukianoff*
> *Director of Legal and Public Advocacy*

For the most part, things would quiet down for the next couple of weeks, until I got an e-mail from a student who had attended a lecture given by Hal White in a "media law" course. White had apparently exercised his First Amendment rights by giving a lecture on the e-mail controversy while substituting for another professor. The student warned me that I needed to be aware of what was being said about me by university administrators in the presence of other students. The student also said that he would come by the office later to talk about it some more. When he did, he said that White criticized both the FIRE and me for "sensationalizing" the e-mail case. He also said that White accused us of trying to "dictate the university's course of action" in the controversy. I didn't worry much about what he said as students sometimes exaggerate things that happen in the classroom.

However, my concerns were later heightened when another student who attended White's lecture called to say that he had lost respect for White for giving an "inappropriate" lecture on the e-mail controversy. I explained to the student that White had every right to fully express his views in a lecture on the topic. After all the negative publicity UNCW was getting, he was understandably eager to defend himself and his actions. The student responded to my defense of White by saying that he was unfairly biased towards the Fullers.

Later that day, I called the FIRE office to ask if the university had ever responded to Lukianoff's November 8th letter. I expressed my concerns about the fact that the university would not defend its actions in any forum other than an audience of undergraduate students. The news that White had criticized FIRE from behind the podium without responding to their letter was poorly received in their Philadelphia office. They responded to White's attack one week before Christmas.

December 18, 2001:

A FIRE press release with the headline "UNCW, Without Shame, Invades Professor's Privacy and Chills Everyone's Free Speech" appeared on www.thefire.org. In the text of the press release, FIRE President Alan Kors criticized the university's action saying, "Administrators at UNC-W apparently have concluded that the senseless demands of one individual— demands that have no legal merit and that the school itself dis- missed at first—are enough to trump the constitutional rights of another. It is a sad case of careerism and indifference to principle." Kors continued, "Rosa Fuller claimed she wanted an 'open discussion,' but when e-mails came to her that were dismissive of her ideas, she quickly abandoned the freedom of speech she claimed to foster. It's as if she believes that speech is only free to the extend to which it agrees with her ideas."

The press release also hammered UNCW for failing to respond to FIRE's original letter. The negative e-mails soon started to pour in from around the country. Provost John Cavanaugh immediately started responding to them but, due to the volume of responses, had to issue a form statement. Apparently hastily constructed, the provost's response would backfire, making matters far worse than they already were. It was a public relations nightmare in the making.

> *Dear _____,*
> *I am writing in response to your e-mail.*
> *Contrary to some reports, Dr. Adams was never investi- gated, threatened, or sanctioned for saying anything by this administration. In fact, the administration on three occasions refused to grant a request filed to us under the Public Records Law of North Carolina seeking blanket access to his corre- spondence. We asked for and received the support of the Attorney General of North Carolina in denying access to Dr. Adams' records to the complainant. We gave our full support*

for Dr. Adams to speak freely on any issue, a point he acknowledged on national television (the Hannity and Colmes show). Even after we were forced to respond to a narrowly framed request for certain records, we did not turn over any records to the requestor because none were relevant. The bottom line is that Dr. Adams has not ever been stifled by this administration, a point he has publicly acknowledged...

... I believe you have been misled by shoddy journalistic reporting by individuals who did not ever check firsthand sources.

John Cavanaugh

That form e-mail was a big mistake. By the time I checked my e-mail later in the week and read what the provost had written, another FIRE press release came out. This time the provost and the chancellor had their pictures posted under a headline which read: "UNCW Shames Itself Yet Again: Provost Responds to FIRE by Denying What Occurred."

In the text of their second press release, FIRE had exposed Provost Cavanaugh for making the following claims about the case: 1) that I was never investigated, 2) that I was never punished for exercising my First Amendment rights, 3) that my expression was not stifled by the university, 4) that UNCW did not turn over any records to my student accuser, 5) that the university was "forced" to comply with the student accusers' requests for documents, 6) that I praised UNCW's actions, and 7) that FIRE never "checked" with them or consulted any primary sources. All of the above claims were demonstratively false and FIRE used UNCW's own internal documents to refute them. The following excerpt from their press release demonstrates just how badly the university was burned in its attempt to cover up its invasion of my privacy:

Releasing student and faculty e-mail records: UNC-

> *W claims that it did not turn over any records to the stu-*
> *dent accuser. In fact, on October 25, University Counsel*
> *Harold M. White, Jr. turned over a printout of the date*
> *and times of all of the e-mails sent by Professor Adams from*
> *September 17-September 18, 2001. The printout, the bot-*
> *tom line of which reads, "Printed for Hal*
> *White...10/22/01," details the identity and e-mail*
> *addresses of everyone with whom Adams communicated,*
> *including nine on-campus and fourteen off-campus e-mails.*
> *A cover letter of October 25, 2001 from University Counsel*
> *White to Fuller, Adams' would-be persecutor, stated: "A list*
> *of these e-mails and the addresses to which they were sent*
> *are attached."...*

From there, things just got worse for the university. The
details of the process of reading the e-mails and inspecting my
computer were described in a way that left few readers in
doubt about whether there had been an investigation that had
the effect of chilling constitutionally protected free speech.
For example, Hal White was quoted directly from university
documents as saying that the process "caused predictable consternation, outrage and a feeling of violation and invasion of
privacy on the part of those whose mail was to be inspected."
Furthermore, to show that I did not defend UNCW's actions,
FIRE referred to the part of the Hannity & Colmes transcript
where I stated that the intrusion exerted a "serious chilling
effect on free speech." In short, they picked apart
Cavanaugh's form denial in a way that made him appear to be
grossly dishonest. It was excruciating to read the entire press
release, which ended by again reminding the reader that most
of the misrepresentations by the university were exposed by
looking at their own internal documents.

I recalled my first conversation with the provost in which I promised to bring out the "big guns" if Dr. Turrisi did not call off her witch hunt. Nonetheless, the university tried to appease everyone in order to avoid bad publicity and a possible (though unlikely) lawsuit. In other words, they had tried to make everyone happy rather than simply doing the right thing.

In the end, my accusers were mad at the university, I was mad at the university, the university was mad at my accusers, the university was mad at me, the press was mad at the university, the FIRE was mad at the university, and so on. In short, the process of trying to please everyone in order to avoid bad press was a miserable failure. It was a public relations nightmare.

Whenever I started to feel bad about the negative PR, I would start to think about the university's denials, and my mood would change to one of outright embarrassment. It truly was a shameful episode, demonstrating a real moral vacuum in our university's leadership. I hoped the whole incident would teach our administrators that they should not do things in private unless they are prepared to defend them in public. Clearly, these were problems that only the First Amendment could resolve.

EPILOGUE

My Application For
Director of Diversity

Dear Selection Committee:

I am absolutely thrilled to hear that the university is considering a new administrative position under the title of Associate Provost of Diversity. I am sure that the current Director of the Office of Diversity will be promoted to that position as soon as it is formally announced. Even though her office has spent over a million dollars on diversity, and the black student population has actually decreased by two percent, I know that she has really tried hard and will be rewarded for her efforts. In fact, I have read that she has even attended conferences in the Bahamas in order to get exposure to innovative ideas on cultural diversity.

I hope that the present director will leave behind the color television set in her spacious office because I have decided to apply for her position. As a conservative, pro-life Republican

and a member of the NRA, you have to admit that I am per-
fect for the job. Who else could bring such a fresh new perspective to an office that has focused solely on left-wing politics for the better part of a decade? In case you aren't convinced, let me tell you more about myself.

My interest in diversity issues began in the Spring of 1993,
when I was applying for teaching jobs and was told by another university that I would probably not be hired by them
unless the other candidate for the position, a black male,
turned down their offer. They said that they had a quota to
meet. I thought that was unfair so I withdrew my candidacy.
Since then, I have sat through job searches at UNCW where
applicants were criticized or rejected because they were "too
white male," "too religious," or "too conservative." As the
new Director of Diversity, I plan to meet with all department
chairs on campus to make sure that kind of thing never happens again at UNCW.

I will also make sure that no one is ever moved up from the
alternate interview list and granted an interview solely on the
basis of his or her race and/or gender. When that happened a
few years ago in my department, a white woman, falsely
claiming to be black, was given an interview she would not
have otherwise been granted. That was wrong and it has to
stop. I will also make sure that the next time we have an event
entitled "The Great Affirmative Action Debate" at UNCW,
there will be two speakers, one speaking for affirmative action
and one speaking against it. The last time we only had the former. That wasn't really a debate, and it wasn't a true reflection
of the spirit of diversity.

When I sat on the Sexual Assault Advisory Board a number
of years ago, one member of the board tried to force fraternity men into a rape awareness program under threat of expulsion if they did not attend. Less than a year later, a colleague

of mine tried to have a male professor fired for arguing that some rapes are more serious than others. As Director of Diversity, I will make sure that different views on the social and legal aspects of rape are respected. Rape is too serious a crime to be used as a device for forcing non-rapists out of our university community.

As Director of Diversity, I will also ensure that all accusations of racism and sexism will be taken seriously on this campus. For example, every time I hear about an accusation of racism, I will personally call the accuser and ask two questions. First, how do you define racism? Second, how does that definition apply to the accusations you are making now? A few years ago, I asked those two questions to a professor who accused me of racism for supporting California's Proposition 187—a bill banning the distribution of government welfare benefits to the families of illegal aliens. The conflict was resolved when he was unable to define racism.

I will also encourage Human Resources to investigate all claims of sexual harassment even when they appear to be unwarranted. If it is determined that a charge has been made in bad faith, the accuser will be punished in order to ensure that true victims of harassment will be taken seriously. Several years ago, when a female professor levied a false harassment charge against her department chair, nothing was done. Later, that same woman filed a false felony charge against him with the university police. Again the charges were unfounded. She still teaches here today.

I also intend to dramatically change the selection of guest speakers at UNCW. For example, the next time that Cornel West speaks at UNCW (for $12,000), I will invite another speaker to explain why it is not morally acceptable to praise the Los Angeles race riots—where whites were dragged out of their vehicles and beaten—as "a justifiable expression of social outrage." The next time Brent Staples speaks at UNCW (for $7,500), I will have another speaker explain why it is bad for race relations when minorities single out white people and chase them down the street in order to make them think they are about to be robbed. Finally, if the Reverend Jesse Jackson ever comes back to UNCW, I will have a speaker come in to explain why it is bad to compare a racist murderer and rapist like Gary Graham to Jesus Christ and Martin Luther King, Jr. Pro-life, pro-gun, fundamentalist, anti-welfare, and anti-affirmative action speakers will also be invited to UNCW in order to make things a little more interesting.

I will also urge the Faculty Senate to have the faculty handbook amended to make it known that every professor—regardless of party affiliation—has a right to put political stickers on his or her office door. The university has far more serious issues to deal with than to review a complaint by a Democratic professor who takes offense at a George W. Bush bumper sticker on a Republican professor's door.

We should also offer First Amendment sensitivity training classes to teach people that there are consequences to expressing your First Amendment rights. For example, if you send a mass e-mail blaming the 9/11 terrorists' attacks on the American government, not on the terrorists, you will probably tick some people off. This is especially likely if you do it only days after the attacks. If people should respond negatively to you, there is no reason to call the police or petition the university to pry into people's e-mail accounts, unless someone specifically threatens you. This rule applies even if your mother is a university administrator. It also applies when someone says they hope a scud missile is fired up your rear end. After all, someone who writes such a message probably doesn't even have a scud missile. Nor do they have the capacity to fire it up your rear end. It's crude, but it's just not a threat.

I also intend to invite UNCW graduate Rosa Fuller back to campus to give a speech entitled "Explaining the Fall of the Berlin Wall Within the Marxist Dialectic." Security guards will be provided. Afterwards, I will give a lecture entitled, "The State May Own the Stalls in the Women's Restroom But Decent People Don't Go Peeking Inside of Them." If that title doesn't fit on the flyers, I will just call it "E-Mail Privacy: It's a Right We Can All Understand."

I also intend to change the way we deal with homosexuals, bisexuals, and cross-dressers. Put simply, we are going to talk about them a lot less. For example, our student orientation leaders are no longer going to have to answer questions about their views on sexual orientation in order to be orientation leaders. Also, when we have gay rights speakers, those introducing them are not going to say that anyone opposed to gay rights is a "homophobe." We will respect the view of Christians who object to homosexuality without characterizing their faith as a disease.

Next, I intend to call for the resignation of Katherine Bell Moore from the UNCW Board of Trustees. Ever since she started making racially charged comments in public, including calling a police officer "white trash," UNCW has lacked the moral authority to discipline white students for directing racial epithets at minority students. That has to stop immediately. We need to stand up for principle, not cave in to the powerful.

I am also going to ask the Women's Resource Center to sponsor three events. The first will be a lecture called "Why the Women's Resource Center is Divisive-and Sexist, Too." The second, will be a showing of the film "The Silent Scream" which will help people to understand (even if they don't accept) the view that abortion is, in fact, murder. Finally, there will be a lecture entitled, "Why We Should Have Asked the Students If They Wanted a Women's Center Before We

Built It." If that doesn't fit on the flyers we'll call it "So What's Next, Separate Water Fountains?" I will also seek the dismissal of any professor who tells a student not to sign up for a class on the basis their gender.

Perhaps most importantly, I will seek to have all speech codes abolished at UNCW. Currently, we promote the idea of diversity at UNCW with affirmative action and a number of other programs. If those programs succeed in bringing people with different views together, we must expect people to get offended from time to time. Therefore, the speech codes are at odds with our larger diversity mission.

My final goal will be to abolish the Office of Campus Diversity. Every professor should know that it is their duty to prepare students to function in our democracy society. They should also know that the United States Constitution is the cornerstone of our democracy. Therefore, we will simply hand each professor a copy of the Constitution, along with their apartment finder packets, when they arrive to teach at UNCW. This will save the taxpayers a lot of money by not having to pay my salary as Director of Diversity. I will probably start a radio talk show after I abolish my job.

I sincerely believe that if I am named Director of Diversity, I will be able to effect changes that will create a climate at UNCW in which more conservative voices can ultimately be heard. I hope you will take this application seriously. I meant every word I said.